The Best Lover, Ever

How to be

The Best Partner

in a Committed,

Monogamous

Relationship

The Best Lover, Ever

Andrew Paul Sokolsky

BIG ISLAND
PRESS

Big Island Press
California, U.S.A.
thebestloverever.com

ISBN 978-0-692-15898-2 (paperback)
ISBN 978-0-692-16374-0 (ebook)

Produced by Page Two
www.pagetwostrategies.com

Dedicated to
the lover within you

Contents

Introduction

WHEN PEOPLE SEE a book titled *The Best Lover, Ever*, some of them assume that it's only about sex. While a satisfying sex life is important, this book is really about how to be the best partner possible in a committed, monogamous relationship. My goal is for you to be your partner's best lover, ever, which means that in the totality of how you communicate with and treat your partner, you're the best for them. I hope you have or will be able to experience a relationship in which you're both happy and content, knowing you made the right choice to be with each other.

I know that you know a lot about love, so I don't presume that you need all of what I recommend. My hope is you will find in this book an idea or two that will enhance your relationship, or, if you're currently single, your next one.

As I wrote this book, I was inspired by the thought that someone I had never met might be influenced by and possibly benefit from my experience and insight. If that person is you, I thank you, as writing this book was one of the great pleasures of my life. I'm honored to believe that something I have to offer might impact your relationship.

I have been in the helping profession for over three decades, as a chiropractor in practice in San Francisco, and as a life coach, supporting people through the many challenges of daily life. I have found that it's easier to solve other people's problems than my own, so writing this book has been beneficial to me. I have been reminded that you earn the blessings of a wonderful relationship on a daily basis, in every action you take.

I have done my best to write a book free of gender and sexual orientation bias. If there are places where, as a heterosexual male, I have used words or phrases that show an unintended bias, please forgive me. My book makes no reference to marriage, although I believe that all married couples are, by definition, partners.

The present moment is always the best time to foster a sense of connection and peace among people. I honor the part of you that expresses love to yourself and to others, and I hope that you have or will have a partner who is, for you, the best lover, ever!

1

The Art of Listening

One of the greatest gifts that you can give to your partner is to truly listen to them. When you genuinely hear your partner, you honor what they have to say, and demonstrate how much you care about them. Listening with attentiveness, respect, and love helps create greater emotional and physical intimacy.

ONE OF THE best ways to develop intimacy in your relationship is to allow your partner to feel the joy that comes with being heard. When you listen attentively to your partner, you will hear them telling you what they desire and how you can fill their needs. If you want your relationship to be as loving and satisfying as possible, do your very best to listen to what your partner is saying.

If your partner believes that you're not listening to them, it gives the impression that you don't care about or respect them. A primary reason that a person thinks about having an affair or ending a relationship is because they feel sadness and shame when they believe that they're not being heard, respected, or appreciated.

Being heard is sometimes the only thing that a person needs, and the listener doesn't need to take further action. Some people have a tendency to jump right into how to "fix" a problem, when the first and most important step is to listen. Sometimes an action or a certain response is needed and sometimes it isn't. Either way, listening attentively lets another person know that you care about them.

It's important to understand the different levels of listening. Have you ever spoken to someone who didn't hear you at all? They're distracted or involved in their own thoughts or actions, and couldn't repeat a word of what you've said or even tell you the subject of the conversation. This is the lowest level of listening.

The second level of listening is when a person you're talking to hears some or all of what you're saying, but then makes the conversation all about them. They essentially ignore what you're saying by making their experiences the center of the conversation. They're either selfish or unskilled at interpersonal relations. Here's an example. You say to a friend, "I'm thinking of breaking up with my boyfriend and I feel sad." They immediately respond, "Two years ago I broke up with my boyfriend and it was really bad. Then I started dating this other guy and I couldn't believe it when he broke up with me! Now, I'm dating a guy who never listens to me. Can you believe that! He's so clueless!"

The third level of listening is far better than the previous levels. By carefully listening to and remembering what someone is saying, you'll be able to repeat back the words that they have spoken. If, for example, your partner says, "Next Tuesday is the parent-teacher conference at 6 p.m., and I want you to go without me. I want to go but I have to work late, again," you can repeat back to them what they said, and ask if you have heard them correctly. When you want to make sure you've heard something clearly, repeat or paraphrase your partner's words, and then ask if you've missed anything.

The highest level of listening includes the ability to remember and repeat, combined with empathy and compassion. It also includes self-awareness: you understand that your judgments, as well as your personal shadows and wounds, may cloud what you hear. With practice, listening attentively with love and care is a skill that you can improve upon. Start by paying attention to the words that a person uses, hearing their tone of voice, and watching their facial expressions and body language. With sensitivity, ask if what you're hearing and judging to be true is correct. Listening at the highest level allows you to genuinely hear another person.

Let's use the parent-teacher conference conversation as an example. Along with making it clear that you understand the request, you might say, "It sounds as if you're upset that you'll be working late that night and can't go to the conference with me. Is this true?" If you know them well enough, you will sense what's behind the words that they're speaking. You may hear the anger in their voice or see the sadness in their facial expressions.

Since you might be wrong, honor them and yourself by asking if you what you believe to be true is correct.

Try to support your partner by respecting whatever their response is, without trying to "fix" the problem or judging their thoughts and feelings. There may be a time for taking action to change certain things, but for now, be as supportive as possible by listening to and hearing what they're saying, and then responding compassionately.

As you listen on a deeper level, you can respond by starting sentences with, "What I hear you saying is," or "I'm getting the impression that," or "What I'm hearing behind the words you're saying is . . ." You might also ask, "Do you feel like I've heard you and I understand what you're saying?" Your goal isn't to be their therapist, but to let them know that you care about and love them, and you're doing your best to understand what they're saying. Ultimately, you hope they feel heard and supported by you.

Sometimes, of course, when they say, "I want to go to the movies," they mean just that and there isn't any hidden or multilayered meaning. As you develop the skill of listening and observing with empathy, love, and as non-judgmentally as possible, it will become much easier to understand your partner and know if there are layers of meaning behind their words.

For some people, listening in this way may not be easy. It may seem as if it takes a lot of effort, but with enough patience and practice, your skills will improve. When you listen at the highest level, it will lead to the two of you forming a deeper emotional and physical connection. When your partner thinks, "I'm very lucky to be in this relationship. I feel cared for and understood. My partner actually listens to me and understands what I want and need," you know you have developed another skill that will allow you to be their best lover, ever.

Recently, a friend told me that the woman she was living with was breaking up with her. Her girlfriend had told her numerous times that she was unhappy and was thinking of moving out. My friend confessed that she'd heard her express her unhappiness, but as is often the case, my friend thought that she had more time to change things and repair the problems in their relationship. This isn't uncommon. Many people in her situation can recall many subtle and overt clues that let them know that the other person was serious about leaving. In fact, the other person often shares their unhappiness many times, giving their partner time to act. One of the keys to not being shocked that the other person has left or has had an affair is to really listen to them, and then take action before it's too late.

Sometimes I hear from a friend or client, "I didn't realize my partner was unhappy. It happened so suddenly." From the person who's leaving I hear, "They never listened to me, they never heard what I was saying, and they never valued what I said enough to do something about it. I told them a hundred times that I was unhappy." Sadly, it's often only after a breakup that people realize how many cues they missed, didn't take seriously enough, or didn't act on.

Even if we practice listening at the highest level, it doesn't guarantee that a relationship will last. However, it does allow us to be aware of problems before they get worse, and it gives us a chance to act in ways that may genuinely address a problem before it's too late.

When you listen at the highest level possible, you have an opportunity to model this skill to your partner and others, and you will be more deserving of your partner's full attention when it's returned to you. If you're not receiving the gift of being heard, first make sure that you're doing your part. Many problems in relationships come from one person waiting for something from the other, without giving it first. If you want to receive the gift of loving and attentive listening, make sure that you give the same to your partner, and there will usually be a shift in the communication between you. As an added bonus, when you give without asking for anything in return, the universe will return your kindness in pleasant ways that may surprise you.

I once read a book for fathers who wanted to communicate better with their teenage daughters. It included a story about a man who, after picking his daughter up from school one afternoon, listened to her talk about anything she wanted to talk about, including her friends, her school, how her day had gone, and whatever else was on her mind. The father listened attentively, nodding appropriately to let his daughter know that she had his full attention. After thirty minutes went by, he hadn't said one word, but she hugged him and said, "Dad, I love you. This is the best conversation we ever had." His attentive, non-judgmental listening gave her exactly what she wanted.

For many people, the sweetest sound is the sound of their own voice. When I give dating advice, I suggest listening attentively on a first date and asking follow-up questions that let the other person know that you're interested in what they have to say, and you're enjoying listening to them. When you listen carefully and give the other person a chance to carry the conversation, they may find you fascinating to be with. By being attentive, you'll learn a lot about your date, helping you decide whether they might be right for you.

In your relationship, frequently let your partner say whatever they want. It's a nice gift that they'll appreciate. You probably receive this gift more often than you realize, and if you don't, you can ask for it.

The other day, I was listening to a person whom I judged to be talking for way too long. As he droned on, I thought to myself, "What can I learn from this man?" The answer was that it's good advice to "listen more and talk less." As you practice becoming a better listener, you will discover the gifts that come from being attentive, including becoming more conscious of your own thoughts.

Sometimes when I'm with my partner or when I'm in a more formal setting giving advice and guidance, I will say to myself, "Be quiet. This isn't the time to talk. This is the time to listen." I then repeat this to myself as often as is necessary, while listening attentively. I believe that by doing this, I become a better advisor, friend, and partner.

When I was a college lecturer, I was responsible for teaching a weekly four-hour class. As I come from a family of teachers, lecturing is in my blood, and it's enjoyable and easy for me. One of the many things I learned from that experience is that for me, it's much easier to talk for four hours than it is to listen for four hours. Many of us are very good at talking, but our listening skills are less developed. Being a caring, attentive listener is essential to being a great conversationalist and partner. When you allow your partner to experience the joy that comes with being listened to, understood, and cared for, they will want to open their heart to you.

2

The "Need to Be Right"

A person's "need to be right" often interferes with their ability to connect with their partner in a way that creates deep emotional intimacy. One partner being right and the other wrong usually creates a distance between partners, rather than bringing them closer. When you honor and respect your partner's opinions, judgments, and points of view, you will nurture a more loving relationship.

Many people have been taught that life is filled with battles that must be won and opportunities that must be seized. They believe that life is a competition and only the strong survive; there are only winners and losers, and "to the victors belong the spoils."

People face off against each other in business, the courtroom, and sporting events, where talent, intelligence, and fierce competitiveness are valued and respected. After the meeting, trial, or post-game celebration, the "loser" often congratulates the "winner," and they honor each other's effort.

If the same type of competitiveness is brought into your relationship, you may discover that what's effective in the world of business or sports doesn't work for you at home. You may get a rude awakening when a "win at all costs" attitude has the opposite effect of what you're hoping to achieve.

A strong need to be right may allow you to get what you think you want, but what have you really won? More importantly, what might you have lost? In your relationship, an argument may erupt as you attempt to prove yourself right, and although you may believe that you've won, the "victory" is often short-lived, hollow, and unfulfilling.

What do you get when you prove yourself right and your partner wrong? It's not the deep connection that comes from truly showing respect and appreciation for each other. In fact, your partner will be less likely to sing your praises or even want to be around you. When they believe that in your eyes they're not smart, or that their thoughts and beliefs aren't respected, your partner may feel sadness, shame, and anger. In turn, they're more likely to distance themselves emotionally and physically from you.

Unfortunately, many people grow up in households where they experience emotional or physical abuse. Others may grow up in homes where there's constant arguing and there always has to be a winner and a loser, or where intellect is valued most, and "the smartest" or "most clever" prevails. I believe that none of these environments provide a good model for the best way to interact with your partner.

Outside the home, if your goal is to persuade a customer to buy something, or to convince someone to share your beliefs, arguing will rarely result in you getting what you want. In the short term, it may feel good to yell and possibly "win" an argument, but the person who's bullied, disrespected, or intimidated into doing something won't feel good about the experience.

Although this method may work once, if this person is given an opportunity to meet with you again, they most likely will steer clear of what they suspect will be another unpleasant experience, and they'll go elsewhere to get their needs met.

When it comes to a professional interaction, try applying the saying, "The customer is always right, but they're not always correct." This saying has served me well through years of service to students, clients, and patients. It helps me to relax as I interact with other people, fulfilling their needs while still honoring myself. What serves me best is not to argue with people or challenge their strong beliefs. While I will speak my truth calmly and clearly, I try to be judicious in the use of argumentative, intimidating, or combative speech, and I try to apply these same guidelines when I'm with my partner.

At home, when you intimidate your partner emotionally, physically, or intellectually in order to be right or to "win" an argument, there's no winner and certainly no reward. If you'd like your partner to feel good when they're with you, and feel safe opening their heart to you, I suggest greatly diminishing or completely letting go of your need to always be right.

I encourage you to honor and respect your partner's opinions, judgments, and points of view. This starts with acknowledging that they have a lot to offer and are worthy of being listened to. Even if you're certain that you're right, you should exercise caution in insisting that your partner should agree with you.

All people want to be listened to and respected. Especially when it comes to establishing a loving and passionate relationship, your willingness to hear and respond with as little judgment as possible diminishes the impulse to make yourself appear smarter or more insightful. It also makes listening to your partner easier, as your mind can be attentive but relaxed. You can then genuinely hear your partner, rather than listening to the voice of your own judgments. How nice it is after a day of hard work, possibly filled with competition and combativeness, to come home and be supportive of each other. A big part of that support comes from putting aside your need to be right at the expense of your partner.

Outside the home, when two people argue in similar ways based on what they consider to be reason, logic, and facts, there's sometimes an acknowledgement that one person is right and the other wrong. One person may even acknowledge that the other has won the argument based on their knowledge, reason, and command of logic. At home, however, a person who's used to interacting in this way may be frustrated when they realize that their partner honors feelings and intuition more than, or as much as, reason, logic, and facts.

If you can recognize and accept that you and your partner may have different values and beliefs, you will be less likely to judge them. It can be useful to remember that their intelligence, wisdom, and ways of communicating with you are some of the reasons that you're attracted to them.

Most situations don't necessitate a winner or loser, or someone being right and the other wrong. In fact, one reason a partner may decide to have an affair or end their relationship is that they feel shame, sadness, fear, and anger when they're consistently disrespected or devalued by being made to be "wrong" while their partner is "right."

What are the roots of a person's need to be right? It could be a need to feel more powerful, which stems from deep-seated insecurities and low self-esteem. The person may be reacting to a sense that their life is out of control. Early childhood wounds may result in a need to control circumstances or dominate another person through words or by force. It's also possible that they have seen this controlling behavior modeled by a parent or other influential adult.

I don't mention these possibilities so that you'll become your partner's therapist. I offer them so that if you find yourself with a powerful need to be right, you will better understand your words and behaviors, or those of your partner.

Tempering your need to be right doesn't mean that you need to hide your feelings, intelligence, intuition, or logical mind. In fact, when these qualities are used to their fullest, you'll get greater insight into what may be motivating your need to be right, and you'll then have less need to prove yourself to others. You may very well find yourself being more accepting and appreciative of your partner.

Through your words and actions, allow your partner to feel the pleasure that comes from being respected and honored, which will create a more loving relationship.

3

Being Kind

Acting with genuine kindness toward your partner is one of the best ways to show that you respect and care deeply for them. Being kind creates a sense of peace and safety that allows you to relax and enjoy each other's company.

HOW YOU TREAT and interact with your partner is a key component of having a loving relationship that will stand the test of time. Kindness includes being thoughtful, considerate, compassionate, appreciative, respectful, good-hearted, and grateful, all qualities that set the stage for true emotional and physical intimacy.

Displaying these character traits doesn't mean that you need to compromise your values, morals, and ethics. You can demonstrate strength while being considerate and compassionate. In fact, the combination of being strong and kind is very appealing.

Treating others with kindness while also practicing self-care is a skill that can be developed, even if it doesn't come naturally to you. While I'm not suggesting that you pretend, I encourage you to demonstrate to your partner the best parts of yourself. If you have been treated compassionately in your past, it will be easier. If not, it can be very healing to treat others, especially your partner, how you wish you'd been treated.

I have seen people break a cycle of selfishness and abuse by learning to care for themselves and their loved ones. This gives me hope for humanity, and confidence to say that even if you haven't always been treated with kindness, it's still possible to treat other people kindly. Aside from being the right thing to do, it will likely make your partner love and trust you more.

Part of being in a healthy relationship is the ability to accept kindness. Some people find that it's easy to be helpful and good to others, but they struggle with allowing others to be generous in return. When you refuse or resist the generosity of your partner, you take from them the joy of giving, and over time they may offer less and less. Be aware of any resistance that you may have to accepting kindness, and find a balance that allows both of you to experience the joy that comes from giving and receiving.

In the beginning of a relationship, people often feel fantastic, and sex can be intense and connecting. Both people may feel wonderful as they experience the pleasure of thinking that they're in love. They may stay together believing that they're right for each other because they equate passion with compatibility and true love. Even if one person believes that the other might be "the one," it takes time for a person's character to reveal itself. Be aware of getting caught up in a whirlwind of emotions, and making a commitment before knowing if your new partner is a genuinely kind person.

Being kind doesn't include being mean, manipulative, inconsiderate, and thoughtless. Be wary of people who initially seem very giving, but who strongly recommend or demand that you isolate yourself from friends and family. This type of controlling behavior by someone who may seem like a nice person is a seductive form of emotional abuse. It's far from the genuine kindness that's desirable in a healthy relationship. Don't allow anyone to treat you badly. Even if there's an initial physical attraction that connects the two of you, find the strength to protect yourself from emotional manipulation.

Being a kind person includes caring about your partner's feelings, being considerate, and honoring reasonable requests. It includes acting in ways that respect the needs of both of you. Be thoughtful about your partner and their life circumstances. What might you do to make their life easier and more enjoyable? What could you do or say to demonstrate your sensitivity to their needs? How can you let your partner know that you're aware of and concerned about their challenges?

Most people thrive when they feel appreciated. I recommend frequently telling your partner how thankful you are to have them in your life, and telling them the many ways in which they bring you happiness. Be sincere and sensitive to their feelings when you do. If you share your reasons for being grateful in a laughing or joking manner, it will significantly decrease or negate the impact of your words.

People feel good when they're shown respect. Although some people are respectful to strangers, coworkers, and friends throughout the day, they forget to honor and respect the most important people in their lives: their partner and themselves. Respect can be shown in different ways. One way is to understand that your partner may have had a difficult day, or be facing challenges that are affecting their behavior.

Your compassion can be conveyed through your words and tone of voice. Compassion includes empathy, which is the ability to understand someone else's feelings, needs, and challenges. When you demonstrate sensitivity to your partner, it allows for a mutual respect that can become one of the pillars of your relationship.

Allow your good-hearted nature to express itself in your communication with your partner. Act in ways that let them know that you care about, understand, and support them.

When you consistently demonstrate that you're thoughtful, appreciative, respectful, and grateful, your partner is much more likely to be relaxed and happy when they're with you, and they'll know that you're worthy of their love and devotion.

4

Speaking Your Truth

Communicating openly and honestly is an essential part of a healthy and loving relationship. You honor yourself and your partner by sharing your thoughts and feelings in a caring and direct manner. When you consistently communicate clearly and truthfully, your partner will know that when you say something, you can be believed.

ABRAHAM LINCOLN, the sixteenth president of the United States, is sometimes referred to as "Honest Abe." It saddens me that we need to celebrate a person for being honest, as if telling the truth were an unexpected and rare occurrence. It would be refreshing if we could assume that when people speak, they're telling the truth. While we are justified in our skepticism when it comes to listening to politicians and others in public life, in our private lives we want to believe that the people we're closest to are honest.

One way to establish and preserve trust in our public and private lives is by consistently being true to our word. Although most of us believe that being candid is important, it seems harder for some people to speak honestly than to lie or tell half-truths. We seemingly get many short-term benefits from lying or being evasive, which reinforces communicating in a way that isn't honest.

In your relationship, you may convince yourself that it's okay to withhold certain pieces of information, and that by doing so you're protecting your partner. In fact, if you're not forthcoming, you're behaving this way primarily to protect yourself. If you omit uncomfortable details or lie when speaking to your partner, you'll presume that they're also untrustworthy, and you'll constantly be questioning the truth of what they say. This isn't a pleasant way to live, and your relationship will ultimately suffer.

Speaking truthfully with your partner includes being candid about your thoughts, feelings, needs, and desires. It means that you care enough about the two of you to be honest with yourself, and then to share with them what's going on within you, revealing yourself in an open and respectful manner. It doesn't include manipulating the facts, or intentionally being vague or confusing.

For some people this will take effort, and it may require them to change the way that they're used to communicating. However, it's worth it! The result of being open and honest can be amazing, as it can create a close, deep bond between you and your partner. When you consistently communicate with honesty, sensitivity, and respect, it allows for love and intimacy to flourish.

A bond of trust can be easily broken. When you're found to be lying, it can be hard to regain the same level of trust. Lingering doubts that are hard to overcome may always remain. Remember that when you tell the truth, you don't have to keep track of the lies you've told. Not long ago I accidentally sent a text to my partner that was meant for my daughter. It was an innocent mistake, but my words could easily have been misinterpreted as a "caught you" moment, revealing that I had been cheating. Because I knew it was an innocent mistake, I was able to laugh it off. Since I was acting honorably, there was nothing for which I could get "caught." If you're concerned that someone might find out about something you did, the best advice I can give is, don't do it in the first place.

When I reach a certain level of closeness in a new relationship, I want us to be monogamous. Once we make this commitment to each other, it becomes very important to me. Because I'm faithful, I expect the same from my partner. If I were unfaithful, it would be understandable if she no longer fully trusted me.

How should a person act in order to establish a reputation for being honest? I've been bringing my car to a great mechanic for almost thirty years. He has a well-deserved reputation for being impeccably honest. How has he gotten this reputation? By earning it in every interaction he has with a customer. He's not only skilled; he will also tell you what needs to be done, what doesn't need to be done, and the consequences of any car-related decision that you make. It's very comforting to have a professional person act this way, especially when I'm putting my life in his hands. When you start out by being open and truthful and remain so in all your interactions, it will pay many dividends that may not be evident at first.

When you speak truthfully, people may not always like what you say, but they'll grow to trust that you always say what's true for you. Remember that your opinions should be shared with sensitivity and compassion. Some people speak their truth with a sledgehammer rather than in a kind and thoughtful manner, and they don't seem to understand why other people get upset or don't praise them for their honesty. The no-nonsense approach that may work well in business or in other situations often has the opposite effect when you use it with your partner. Yes, speak your truth, but do it in a way that brings you closer, rather than creating distance between you.

It's important to differentiate your truth from "the truth." Few things are "absolutely true." When you share your beliefs, you're stating what's true for you, which is usually a mix of feelings, opinions, and judgments. When you're willing to accept your truth as your own and not as an absolute truth, you open yourself to considering another person's thoughts, feelings, and judgments, without believing that you're right and they're wrong. When you understand that your perspective doesn't need to be accepted as gospel, you're likely to find a much more welcoming and loving partner.

When your partner is being honest and open, give them the opportunity to speak, and do your best to hear what they're saying. If they believe that there's no room to be heard, or you'll only respond by being angry, they'll likely begin to distance themselves emotionally from you. When one or both partners withdraw, it can take a lot of effort to reconnect. Over time, one or both may forget the reasons that they distanced themselves, but feelings of sadness and resentment will linger.

When you let your partner speak their truth and are willing to accept and respect their judgments as being true for them, it gives them a chance to be heard and honored. Even if the two of you disagree, demonstrating respect by listening to each other will further strengthen your bond.

There's a saying that "trust is earned, not given." Upon first meeting someone, most people genuinely want to take the other person at their word. However, many people have become jaded as a consequence of difficult experiences, and they're wary and distrusting of people they don't know. When a relationship starts, being consistently honest allows the other person the chance to more quickly trust and feel close to you. If you continue being open and honest, your potential partner will know that they're with someone special, and the relationship will have a much better chance of flourishing.

When I was a boy and asked my mother a question, there were times when she'd reply, "Do you want to know the truth, or should I lie to you?" She was saying that I might not enjoy hearing the truth, and she could make up an answer that at least in the short term would make me feel better. While I don't think it necessary to share every thought or feeling that you experience, I believe that it's important to be forthcoming and share your truth, even if it results in one or both of you experiencing unpleasant emotions.

There are potential challenges when communicating truthfully. It may be time-consuming, detract from something fun, or interrupt a busy schedule. It may be difficult to discuss what you're thinking and feeling, so ignoring issues may seem simpler and less disruptive to your lives. Communicating openly may shed light on aspects of your relationship that are emotionally painful, and that if talked about could possibly threaten your relationship. While being honest is difficult and you may justify to yourself why the timing isn't right, withholding your truth isn't worth the cost.

Beware of delaying open communication by thinking, "I'm waiting for the right time to talk. When we're having fun, talking about a serious subject ruins the mood. When things aren't going well, talking about this will only make things worse. Let's have this discussion at another time." Unless you think that a discussion should be forever delayed, either set a time to talk, or acknowledge that the present moment is the best time to share what you're thinking and feeling.

If you don't speak your truth, or if you tell a lie in order to avoid possible painful feelings, it sets you both up for more challenges as your relationship progresses. The truth sometimes hurts, but not as much as being lied to by someone whom you love and trust. As in many situations, the crime is usually not as bad as the cover-up.

I know couples that were together for many years before one of the partners had an affair. When the truth was finally disclosed, the relationships were able to survive and ultimately thrive, but only with significant emotional pain for everyone involved. While there are always many factors involved, it's likely that prior to the affair, one or both people weren't sharing their unhappiness, weren't hearing their partner, or weren't willing to make changes. Painful situations such as dealing with the aftermath of infidelity demonstrate the importance of speaking honestly and making sure your partner hears what you're saying. Speaking your truth can be difficult and emotionally painful, but not as painful as the suffering caused by taking an action that you'll ultimately regret. Acting honorably and being open prevents a snowball effect that can have devastating consequences.

When you share your feelings, opinions, and judgments clearly, honestly, and respectfully, your communication will become more intimate and loving, and your relationship can thrive.

5

Expressing Your Emotions

The ability to express what you're feeling respectfully is a very attractive quality that helps create a sense of trust and intimacy in your relationship. Being open and honest about your feelings without blaming others demonstrates sensitivity, strength, and emotional maturity.

In a relationship, one or both individuals may complain that their partner is moody, distracted, or hiding something from them. We sometimes assume that the other person doesn't care about or want to be with us anymore, is no longer attracted to us, or is having an affair.

Most of the time, none of these assumptions are true. Usually the reason for the breakdown in communication is that one or both partners aren't recognizing, acknowledging, honoring, or respectfully communicating their emotions. Developing or improving these skills is well worth it and allows for a much happier relationship.

Recognizing Your Feelings

A healthy expression of feelings starts with an admission to yourself that you're experiencing something in the emotional/feeling realm. For many people this is a big first step. Many young children are taught to ignore or suppress their feelings. They may have been teased and shamed for expressing their emotions, and told that communicating their feelings is a sign of weakness.

"Don't be a cry baby," "suck it up," and "don't act like a child" are unsupportive expressions that many young people hear. They may then unknowingly absorb these negative messages into their personalities and behaviors. When children are taught early in life to ignore what they're feeling, as they move into adolescence and adulthood, it becomes difficult for them to identify or accept what they're feeling, or to understand that their feelings are worthy of being honored and expressed.

One way to make it easier to recognize feelings is to put them in one of six "feeling groups." The group headings are Mad, Sad, Glad, Fear, Shame, and Guilt. Most words used to describe a feeling can fit within one or more of these groups. Thus, I encourage you to use words that you think best describe your feelings, but ultimately to recognize that you're probably feeling either mad, sad, happy, afraid, ashamed, guilty, or a combination of these emotions. You might say to yourself: “I recognize that I’m angry,” “I recognize that I’m sad,” or “I recognize that I’m sad and angry.”

Anger (mad) is a legitimate feeling, especially when expressed healthfully. I grew up in an environment where I experienced many expressions of love, but anger was expressed in unhealthful ways as a withdrawal of affection or as rage. Unfortunately, many people express anger as verbal rage or through an act of violence, without having consciously realized that they were angry until after the damage has been done.

Other feelings are often hidden by the expression of anger. You may feel sadness, shame, guilt, or fear, but it’s knowingly or unknowingly covered up and unexpressed. Through therapy, coaching, or on your own, hopefully you will learn to healthfully express angry feelings and be able to recognize other feelings that may be covered up by anger.

Joy (happiness, peace, pleasure) is at times not recognized or acknowledged. Some people have been taught that the experience of joy should be minimized or hidden. When they experience joy, they may quickly put themselves in a situation where they’re unhappy, as a way of coping with a feeling that may for a variety of reasons be uncomfortable for them to experience. Recognizing how they respond to joyful feelings can start to break the pattern that limits them to only experiencing momentary or short-term happiness.

For many people, expressing gratitude increases their happiness, and “counting their blessings” can create joyful feelings that are less dependent on circumstance. The recognition of how fortunate one is to be alive often creates joy.

Fear can help us survive in what's sometimes a hostile world. It can be liberating when you allow yourself to recognize fear, as doing so sometimes decreases the intensity of this emotion, and may result in you taking the actions necessary to address what's causing your fear. If nothing else, recognizing this emotion (as with other emotions) can be healing.

Shame is the feeling that often results from someone belittling you, or convincing you that you're "less than," or not as important as, other people. Shaming often starts when another person ridicules you, and over time, as their message becomes internalized, your own voice continues the shaming. For example, when you were young, someone may have given you the message that you weren't smart or worthy, and that you would never be good enough. When you get older, you may still hear their voice or possibly your own voice giving you those same messages. It's important to recognize shameful feelings and uncover where the original shaming voices came from.

Guilt is a feeling that often arises when a person speaks or acts contrary to their moral code, which is their sense of right and wrong. When a person violates rules that they or others have set, they're violating an ethical code, and they may also experience guilt.

Sadness is a feeling that some people have a hard time recognizing. They may believe that they don't have the right to feel sad because their external circumstances appear to be very good. Or they may think that it isn't acceptable for them to admit feeling sad, because they were taught that others have it much worse than they do. Some children are taught not to cry and to "put on a happy face," or that sadness is a sign of weakness. I'm continually surprised to hear many people say that as adults, they never cry. Crying can be healing, and for some, it brings a feeling of relief and serenity. Recognizing your sadness is an important first step in accepting it as a legitimate feeling.

Acknowledging Your Feelings (To Yourself)

For some people, recognizing that they're capable of feeling is a new experience. For those people, the next step is identifying what they're feeling. While doing so, it's important for them to acknowledge that they may experience more than one feeling at the same time, and to say to themselves, for example, "I feel angry, but what's behind or underneath my anger is sadness," or "I feel angry, and along with the anger I'm feeling sadness and shame."

To better identify feelings, it's important to make the distinction between a thought and a feeling. A person might say, "I feel like going to the store" or "I feel like eating at that restaurant." Those aren't feelings. A healthier and more accurate expression of feelings would be "When I buy things I want at the store, it makes me feel good [joy]. If I don't buy the things that I want, I will feel disappointed [sad] and frustrated [angry]."

Use the words "angry," "sad," "happy," "afraid," "ashamed," "guilty," or a combination of these to describe and thus acknowledge your feelings. You might say, "When I do this or go there, I feel happy," or "When they yell at me, I feel angry, sad, and ashamed."

When acknowledging your feelings, know that your feelings don't need to "make sense" or be "appropriate" for a given situation. It's fine to think, "I don't know why I'm feeling angry, but I am," or "I should be feeling happy, but I'm feeling sad and fearful." At this stage, you're acknowledging what you're feeling, which lays the foundation for the next important steps of honoring and expressing your feelings.

Honoring Your Feelings

"Honor" is a powerful word. Some of us honor others but not ourselves. You respect yourself by recognizing and acknowledging your feelings. When you say, "I'm worthy of having feelings whether they make sense or not," you're honoring yourself.

Some people believe that their feelings are of little importance. They may believe that their feelings aren't as important as those of their partner, or anyone else. They then put others' needs before their own, and end up feeling angry, sad, ashamed, or a combination of these feelings when their own needs aren't met. A way of demonstrating self-respect is to verbalize that your feelings are worthy of being honored. You demonstrate self-worth when you recognize, acknowledge, honor, and then express your emotions to others.

Expressing Your Feelings (To Another Person)

One partner may say to the other, "You never tell me how you feel," "Don't you feel anything?" or, for some, the dreaded, "Let's talk about our feelings." Perhaps you're the one saying this or something similar, or maybe you're the one hearing it. An attempt by one partner to get the other to open up, even when it's done with good intentions, can turn into a discussion in which one or both people end up feeling angry, sad, or ashamed. Thus, it's important that both partners act and speak in a respectful way, so that their hearts open and the expression of feelings can create a stronger bond between them.

Relationships are a fertile ground for learning. We're often triggered (experience strong emotions) by a word or phrase our partner says, a look they give us, or something they do. We may also experience strong emotions when we judge that they're not saying or doing what we want, expect, or hope for. Upon reflection, our emotional reaction may seem out of proportion to what was said or done, but in the moment, we overreact. As a result of a "backlog" of unprocessed emotions and experiences, we respond in a way that has little or nothing to do with the current situation.

Emotions don't have to be "legitimate" or "valid" in order for you to honor and express them. We often have feelings that don't make sense, at least upon initial examination. You might say to your partner, "I'm not blaming you, but I want you to know that I'm feeling angry and fearful. I know that my response may seem out of proportion to what happened. I'm grateful that I can share my feelings with you." Expressing emotions that don't seem to make sense, if it's done without blaming your partner, reduces the chance that they'll withdraw. It also gives them a chance to support you through what may be a difficult time.

If you're willing to take responsibility for your feelings, and explore the underlying reasons that something your partner says or does results in strong emotions for you, and then you healthfully express your feelings, your relationship will benefit greatly.

With support from a therapist, coach, partner, or on your own, you may be able to understand the reason(s) that specific words, tones of voice, or actions trigger a certain response within you. When you do this, you're more likely to understand your responses and take responsibility for your feelings, thoughts, and actions. A greeting card I bought recently summed it up and made me laugh. It said, "Just Because I'm Blaming You, It Doesn't Mean It's Your Fault."

As mentioned earlier, many people are unaware of their emotions or don't know how to express them healthfully. Thus, we live in a world where acts of violence are far too common. I believe that we would have less violence in our society if we were more willing and better able to recognize, acknowledge, honor, and then express our feelings in a healthy way.

In a relationship, an emotional distance can be created when one or both people don't respectfully express their feelings. One or both partners may think that the other person doesn't understand or care about them.

The good news is that maturely sharing your emotions, and truly caring for your partner, creates a joyful, intimate bond.

When talking with your partner, express your feelings honestly, gently, directly, and respectfully. Showing respect includes listening to and hearing what another person is saying. It includes speaking openly, being kind, not blaming others, and taking responsibility for your emotions. It helps to start sentences with "I feel" or "When this happens, I feel." When you use these expressions, you take ownership of your feelings, which is an attractive quality. When you take responsibility for how you feel, you're exercising your power. By contrast, when you start a sentence with "You make me feel," you give away your power to the other person and try to make them responsible for your feelings. Ultimately, you're responsible for your feelings and for how you respond to your partner.

When speaking, demonstrate respect by using a calm voice. Your tone should convey understanding and affection. People don't like someone else using harsh words, angry tones, or an aggressive body posture when trying to make their point. If you bully your partner by yelling or using an intimidating tone of voice, the intimacy you're trying to cultivate will be lost.

As discussed in chapter 2, "The 'Need to Be Right,'" you honor your partner by not making yourself right and them wrong, and by not turning your communication into a contest to see who wins. The goal of your communication should be to achieve a healthier and more loving connection between you. Honoring your partner includes listening without interrupting and genuinely trying to hear what's being said, rather than planning your response while the other person is talking.

Speaking honestly shouldn't include being harsh, mean, or cruel. Speak clearly and respectfully so that the other person is able to really hear you. It's important to remember that although you're being honest, it doesn't mean that you're correct.

Speak without disguising what you mean. Sometimes people expect others to read their minds and understand their code words or half-truths. They may use analogies, metaphors, and parables, or otherwise use words as a way of hiding from their feelings. They'll beat around the bush, afraid of another person's reaction if they honestly express themselves.

You can be direct while speaking gently. Gentle communication is a sign of respect, and it conveys your message in a way that makes your partner more likely to hear you, and to take comfort in knowing that you don't lose control, or speak in a threatening tone. Many powerful communicators in history spoke softly, with great effect. A friend of mine who worked at a shelter for abused women has a T-shirt that reads, "Gentle Lovers Last Longer." I always liked this message. Remember that the goal is to create a connection between the two of you that naturally leads to greater emotional and physical intimacy.

6

Giving Compliments

When your partner receives acknowledgment and praise, they're likely to open their heart to you. This is especially true if you compliment them about something they value highly. Expressing genuine admiration for your partner creates a more intimate connection between you.

IT'S TRULY SPECIAL and rewarding to bring joy to another person by helping them feel great about themselves. If your partner hears words that encourage and support them, they're much more likely to feel close to you. One of the most important life lessons I have learned is that we don't want to spend time with another person because of how great that person is, but because of how we feel about ourselves when we're with them. When you contribute to another person feeling really good about themselves, they're much more likely to want to be in your company.

As a teenager, I grew up with friends who would constantly insult each other, which at the time was a form of male bonding. However, when it comes to fostering emotional and physical closeness in your romantic relationship, immature verbal assaults that may have been part of your youth are certainly not the best approach. Unfortunately, some people treat their partners as they were treated while growing up, and come off as immature. Many of these people haven't been on the receiving end of enough genuine compliments; if they had, it might have inspired them to act more appropriately.

My father used to say that there are only two types of people in the world who like compliments—men and women. Giving a compliment is an art that combines what you say, how you say it, and when you say it. When you deliver a genuine and sincere compliment in the appropriate manner and at the appropriate time, your partner will be much more likely to respond to you in wonderful ways.

Even if you understand the value of correctly delivered compliments, it's important that you compliment your partner for the right reasons. The goal should not be to get what you want. The goal should be to help your partner feel the joy that comes with being acknowledged and appreciated.

If your compliment is insincere, most people will sense or recognize it. The best thing to do is to base your compliment on something that you genuinely like or admire about the person. For example, don't say that you like a person's sweater if you don't like it. However, you might like their shoes, hat, hair, or whatever! Look at and listen to a person and think about what you admire about what they're wearing, saying, or doing, and tell them.

Compliment them without adding a qualifier, such as "but" or "if only," which devalues whatever was said and may insult the other person. When you use "but" or "if only" at the end of a supposed compliment, what the person on the receiving end hears you saying to them is, "You're not good enough."

For example, yesterday I said to someone close to me, "You're very intelligent, and with all your experience you're sure to find the right job for you." I could tell that the compliment was received and appreciated, and I could see that she experienced joy and pride. My compliment was given genuinely and sincerely. Now, if I had said, "You're very intelligent, and with all your experience you're sure to find the right job, but are you certain you're not talking too much during the interview?" or "You're very intelligent, and with all your experience you're sure to find the right job, if only you had the right clothes to wear," the person on the receiving end of those words would very likely hear, "I think you talk too much and you're not good enough" or "You don't dress well and you're not good enough." Adding any qualifier when giving a compliment defeats its intended purpose. It's as if you were holding out something nice, and then snatching it back at the last moment.

Another example would be the compliment "I like your hat." When you say this, the other person can feel good about their looks or their ability to choose nice things. If you were to say, "I like your hat, but I think that blue would be a better color for you. Don't you agree?" you insult their color choice and imply that they would be better off if they followed your recommendation. On top of that, you then ask them to agree with you! Choose your words with care and sensitivity, as they can either build someone up or tear someone down.

Be aware of "going over the top" with a compliment and sounding insincere. Have you ever received a compliment that sounded untrue even though it was sincere and was meant well? For example, a person says, "That's the most beautiful shirt I have ever seen. It's far and away the nicest one, ever. I mean it!" Another example might be, "I have heard a lot of people say a lot of things, but that's the most insightful statement I have ever heard." Sometimes an exuberant person means what they're saying, but they run the risk of seeming disingenuous.

Find an appropriate way to make the same messages ring true. You could say, "That's a very handsome shirt" or "You made an excellent point in an elegant way. I appreciate your style." Be complimentary in a way that allows a person to feel good, and to trust that what you're saying is genuine.

As in many situations, timing is everything. Be sensitive to the appropriate time to deliver a compliment to ensure that it's received well. If in the middle of an argument, you say, "Wow, your hair looks really good," don't be surprised if it doesn't have the desired impact. You may be trying to shift the mood, but if the other person is experiencing anger or other unpleasant feelings, they probably won't be very receptive to what you're saying.

Also, be sensitive to how people may react when you give a compliment. Sometimes a compliment is best delivered in private. Here's an example that illustrates my point. A man is with his partner, her sisters, and her friends. In front of the entire group he says to his partner, "You're the most beautiful woman, ever." While this is perhaps a wonderful thing to say in private, in this situation it may be embarrassing to his partner, or insulting to the other women. When it's not clear when to deliver a compliment, err on the side of discretion.

A person's tone of voice is often more powerful than their words. Love, kindness, and appreciation can be conveyed through tone. When you're speaking, people can usually sense when you're being truthful. When you combine what you say with a tone that conveys honesty and sincerity, your compliment will be much more impactful.

Be aware that your partner may be sensitive to you complimenting someone else. For example, a man may experience shame, sadness, or anger if right in front of him, his partner tells another man how handsome he looks. The person giving the compliment may wonder why their partner seems unusually quiet, distant, or angry afterwards. Be sensitive to your partner's feelings, and be cognizant of what you say and when you say it.

Give a compliment because it's deserved and appropriate, and do it in a way that helps the other person feel valued. Don't give a compliment in order to hear one in return, or to get a certain response. When this is your intent, it devalues what you're saying and sets you up for disappointment. Over time, compliments will naturally come your way when you practice loving communication.

It's nice to compliment *how* someone does something. Examples of giving a compliment about your partner's style could include the following: "You act with such integrity. I appreciate that," "You handle situations with such grace," "The way you hold me makes me feel safe," or "You treat everyone with such respect. I admire your kind and gentle manner."

Even if your partner knows that you love them, I encourage you to share with them the many things that make them so special to you. I recommend expressing your compliments generously, appropriately, truthfully, and with love. If you're asking yourself if you're giving your partner enough compliments, you're probably not. I once heard a man being asked how often he told his partner how handsome he was. He responded, "Every day." I thought that was the perfect answer!

7

Living with Integrity

When your words and actions are an honest reflection of your thoughts and feelings, and you act honorably while being true to yourself, you're living with integrity. When you live in this manner, people will know that you're sincere in your communication and principled in your actions, and your partner will feel the joy that comes with being able to count on and trust you.

LIVING WITH INTEGRITY is one of the hardest and most satisfying ways to live. When you're honest with yourself about your thoughts and feelings, speak your truth, and act in alignment with what you believe to be right, you distinguish yourself as a person who's principled and trustworthy. Although living with integrity may challenge your relationship, it can result in a bond between you and your partner that's stronger than you thought possible.

For many people, the commitment to live with integrity often presents a choice between short-term comfort and doing what they believe to be right. I judge that most people know the right action to take at every moment of their lives, but they either cloud the truth with rationalizations or make decisions that only provide relief in the moment.

Living with integrity presents challenges that we sometimes seek to avoid. Doing what you consider to be right means that others may not like your words or actions. When you choose to do what's right rather than what's acceptable to others, it's possible that you may no longer be part of "the gang." Taking the right action, when it goes against the thinking of a group, family, or partner, may leave you ostracized and on the outside looking in, which can result in feeling sad and afraid.

Living with integrity may challenge your relationship, but it also gives you the opportunity to have an incredibly powerful and loving connection, where your partner knows that you're courageous and trustworthy.

The benefits of living with integrity are numerous. It will give you an inner strength and a sense that you're fulfilling your purpose, which is very rewarding. Living in alignment with what you believe to be right will put a smile on your face, calm your heart, and bring peace to your soul. It will decrease anxiety, for when your actions flow from your truth, many inner battles and struggles are reduced or eliminated. When you speak and live your truth with dignity and respect for yourself and others, you become a more honorable friend, coworker, family member, and partner.

With all those benefits, it seems like a straightforward choice. Yet, the following reasons may be behind our unwillingness to act with integrity:

- Fear of loss and abandonment
- A sense of vulnerability and anxiety
- Belief that we are dependent on another person
- Desire for financial or emotional stability
- A perceived need to protect ourselves, and our loved ones
- The thought that we may never be in another relationship
- Fear of ending up alone, without companionship

With these reasons in mind, it's easier to understand why living in a principled and honest manner is a challenging choice. In the short term, it may be more challenging to act in alignment with what you believe to be right. Yet the decision not to act with integrity often has a snowball effect with painful long-term consequences, as one seemingly "easy" bad choice leads to another and then another. Sometimes we're not aware that the choice that we've made not to live with integrity has resulted in circumstances that have taken a toll on our happiness and our spirit.

It's difficult to know whether where we find ourselves in life is a result of personal choice, chance, predestination, or a combination of these and other factors. It's best to act and speak honestly and openly, to express your truth gently and respectfully, and to make the choices that you think are right and honorable. As much as is possible, let your life become a reflection of choosing to live with integrity. I believe that living with integrity will keep or invite the ideal partner into your life.

Living with integrity doesn't mean that you're a weak or ineffectual person. It means that you "walk your talk," doing your best to live in a way that reflects your thoughts, desires, values, and principles. It means that you try your best to be true to yourself and to act honorably. It means living up to your commitment to fidelity as it concerns both physical and emotional intimacy. It includes being honest and open about issues that you believe need attention, and being upfront if you're unhappy.

When your partner trusts that you will be honest and faithful, they can more easily commit themselves to your relationship. If you regularly communicate openly with each other, you give yourselves time to address challenges before they become too big to handle. Rather than pretending that there are no issues or problems, if you live with integrity you will address these concerns more quickly, giving both of you a chance to do what's best for your relationship.

One of the ways that I measure my integrity is by observing how I act when I know that no one else is looking, and I will not be seen or "caught" by anyone else. There are a number of ways to measure your honesty and decency. One test is asking yourself whether you would cheat on your partner if you knew that your infidelity wouldn't be discovered. Hopefully, the answer is an emphatic "no."

While none of us are perfect, I recommend doing your best to live with integrity in your relationships with your partner, family, friends, coworkers, and anyone else you have contact with. Although it may seem like a challenging way to live, I believe that it will serve you and others. People will sense that what you do, and the way you carry yourself, is of value.

Act with integrity if you find yourself tempted to seek emotional satisfaction from someone other than your partner, when you know that those needs should be met within your relationship. If you're honest with yourself, you'll experience a sense of unease when you look to others to fulfill needs that should be met by your partner.

I hope that you want to earn and keep a reputation for being open and honest, trustworthy, and faithful. Earlier in my life, when I would find myself unhappy in relationships, I would often not disclose the depth of my unhappiness. At those times, I was not sharing my truth with my partner. I acted as if I was happy when I wasn't, and I now see this as an example of living out of integrity. I have now reached the point in my life where I refuse to be unhappy for long periods of time. I speak my truth and tell my partner that I will never cheat, but that if either of us is unhappy, I want it brought into the open so that we can do what we can to meet each other's needs in a way that satisfies both of us. By communicating this way, I judge that I'm living in integrity with my partner and myself.

For many people their reputation is very important. They do their best to live kindly and generously in alignment with their values. Unfortunately, some people don't live with integrity even though they care about how others think of them. They act very differently from the way that they want to be perceived. We too often see this behavior from people in public life who don't act with integrity, while doing everything to convince us that they're to be respected and admired.

Don't be dissuaded by the constant barrage of news about people who don't seem to know the definition of integrity. Do your best to live in a way that makes you proud of who you are and how you act.

I believe that the truth rarely stays hidden. In the long run, the easiest way to a gain a reputation as a person with integrity is to act sincerely, honorably, and in a principled manner. Do your best to live this way, especially as it relates to your partner. Live in such a way that if the truth about you were known, you would be proud that your thoughts, feelings, behaviors, actions, and ways of communicating were in alignment.

Your feelings can be a guide for how to act in life. Ask yourself, "Do I experience a sense of calm when I behave in a certain way? Do I sense feelings of sadness, shame, or guilt because in my heart I know that I'm not acting with integrity? Am I fearful that my actions may be revealed to someone else? Would I be at peace if people I respect knew the truth about what I'm doing?" When you pay attention to how you feel in response to these questions, it will help you to know if you're acting with integrity.

Two other questions that will reveal a lot are: “If my partner were acting toward me with the same level of integrity that I’m displaying toward them, would I be pleased?” and “Does the way in which I’m living and interacting with others give me a sense of peace in my heart and soul?”

Living with integrity in your relationship includes being open and honest when expressing your emotions, keeping your agreements, speaking your truth, and doing all this in a kind and loving manner. It may seem like a lot of effort, but it’s well worth it.

8

Expressions of Love

Loving and being loved is one of the sweetest pleasures in life. Frequently expressing devotion to your partner allows your relationship to thrive. When you express your affection through your words and actions, life is more fun and exciting, and your intimacy and passion will flourish.

EXPRESSING YOUR LOVE though words, gestures, behaviors, and actions is a vital part of a beautiful relationship. One of the sweetest things a person can hear from their partner is "I love you." When you give voice to your feelings and express your devotion, it tells your partner that they're very special to you. If you're fortunate enough to have found someone who's right for you, frequently demonstrate your affection.

It's amazing what people are capable of when inspired by love. People blossom in unexpected and beautiful ways. Songs that used to sound trite now have meaning. Colors appear more vibrant. Everyone seems friendlier and the world is seen in all its glory. When you're in a relationship, do your best to keep this wonderful feeling alive by frequently expressing your desire and love for your partner.

Some people say that since their partner already knows how much they care, they don't need to express their affection with any regularity. They may say, "You know how I feel about you. Why do I need to tell you?" or "If I don't love you anymore, I will let you know." Neither of these is acceptable. People who use these or similar expressions may be out of touch with their own feelings, or they may be uncomfortable expressing them. It may be difficult for them to communicate affection because in childhood they experienced too few expressions of love.

People who struggle to express their feelings may mistakenly believe that it's acceptable to withhold verbal expression of their love. They may display their affection only with an unspoken action and believe that's enough to demonstrate their devotion. Fixing the car, taking out the garbage, preparing dinner, or doing the dishes are often welcome and appreciated parts of being in a relationship, but they're not, by themselves, expressions of love. Don't assume that because you do important or nice things, your partner knows how much you love them. Even something critical such as taking care of children or other family members isn't in and of itself an expression of love for your partner.

When a person struggles or chooses not to express their affection openly or frequently enough, their partner may quietly yearn for deep and loving communication. It's sad when one or both people don't express their affection for the other, even though it's real and heartfelt. Do what it takes to let your partner know what you're feeling, and sincerely express your thoughts and emotions. Express your love directly to them and do it often. Do it before it's too late and they have left and found someone who will tell them what they long to hear.

One of the most unsettling and problematic things that a partner can say is, "If you loved me, you would know what I'm feeling and thinking, and what I need." Most people aren't mind readers; although you can hope that your partner will pick up on clues and remember your likes and dislikes, placing unrealistic expectations on them isn't fair, and will eventually create problems. Tell your partner what's meaningful to you. You're very deserving of appreciation and devotion, but don't expect another person to read your unspoken thoughts about what makes you feel special.

Hopefully, you will never hear or say, "When was the last time you said you loved me?" or "Please tell me that you love me." These are words that you may hear shortly before one of you says, "I think we should break up" or "I met someone else." People often think that they have more time than they actually do to heal problems in a relationship. I'm not saying that by offering expressions of appreciation and affection, all your problems will be resolved. However, if you're able to keep your relationship as satisfying and enjoyable as possible, there's less of a chance the relationship will need to be "rescued." Regularly demonstrate your love through your words and actions, and let your partner know the joy they bring to your life.

It's very important to know what makes your partner feel cared for and cherished. For example, let's say you have decided to do something very special to show how much you love your partner. You decide to demonstrate your affection by cleaning the kitchen floor, which is something you don't usually do. You even go to the store and buy new cleaning supplies to make sure that you do a great job. The store doesn't have what you want, so it takes longer than you expected to get the required items, but that's okay because you feel energized by the thought that you're doing something special. You're glad that they're not home yet because it's a big job and it will take time and a lot of effort, but they're worth it!

Your partner gets home and doesn't even notice the clean floor, so you decide to show them because you're looking forward to their reaction. They don't seem very enthusiastic or appreciative of your efforts. You may feel confused, sad, and angry. What's going on? Are they mad at me? Don't they love me? What's most likely going on is that they're not expressing appreciation and gratitude for all your hard work because they're thinking, "For me, cleaning the floor isn't an expression of love."

If instead of cleaning, you met them at the door with a hug and kiss, told them how much you love them, and asked if they would like to go to dinner at their favorite restaurant, this expression of affection might be the right combination that makes them feel loved. By asking, experimenting, observing, and being sensitive to your partner's needs and desires, you will gain a much better sense of what makes them feel cared for and loved.

If you're unsure of what's meaningful to your partner, ask them. You can also ask yourself, "What's unique about my partner? What do they like to do? What do they value? What brings them joy? Based on what I know about them, what makes them feel great?"

Along with figuring out what gestures are meaningful to them, think about what makes you feel special. For me, when an anniversary, holiday, or birthday comes along, what I want more than a gift is a card filled with tender and heartfelt sentiments. I realize that fancy gifts and diamonds bring some people joy. Or maybe it's getting to sleep on the side of the bed that they like best. Maybe it's picking the movie that they want to see. Everyone is unique. The point is, if both of you communicate what makes you feel appreciated and special, it will be much easier to give and receive expressions of love that create the special connection you desire.

By carefully listening to your partner and remembering what's important to them, you can create intimacy through seemingly small gestures. A couple I know who are committed to each other but don't live together, always text each other good morning and good night. These texts are symbolic of their commitment to each other, and are a sweet way of saying that they're thinking of each other when they wake up and before they go to sleep. This gesture has a lot of meaning for them, to the point where when one of them did not text "good morning" for two days in a row, they talked about whether there was a problem in their relationship that they needed to address. As it turned out, it was due to completely innocent circumstances. Couples often have special ways of connecting that have meaning only to them. Little things can make a big difference, so find out what has meaning for both of you, and let seemingly small gestures carry a very loving message.

Politeness and courtesy are important, and they're also nice ways of expressing how much you care about your partner. For example, when my partner and I take my car, I open the passenger side door for her, make sure that she's comfortably seated, and then gently close the car door. While this may seem old-fashioned, I find that it's much appreciated. I always hold doors for her and make other courteous gestures—not in a condescending way, but as a way of demonstrating my affection and respect for her. There's no expectation on my part, and she appreciates these gestures.

While you can of course be nice to anyone, it's especially important that you be good to your partner. Sometimes we treat everyone else better than those we care about most. If you're guilty of this, hopefully it's not too late to change. If your partner seems to turn elsewhere to get their needs met, do what you can to become the person they most want to turn toward. Expressions of love, as a regular reminder of how much you care about them, help keep you front and center when they want support and comfort.

Please know that it's never okay for someone to say, "I love you," and then behave abusively. Abusive behaviors aren't expressions of love, and nothing can change this truth. No combination of words or gifts can compensate anyone for being treated badly. There are many potential partners out there who will want to treat you well and be generous with their affection. If you're being emotionally or physically abused, it's time to end your relationship and find someone who's deserving and respectful of you.

Ideally, giving a gift to your partner demonstrates that you know and care about them. When gifts are thoughtful, they make a huge impact. In a typical 1950s or 1960s TV show, the boss instructs his secretary to buy a gift for his wife that he can then present to her as if he'd bought it. Let me be straightforward and tell you that's not okay. Listen carefully so you know what gifts your partner would like to receive. This takes effort for some people, but it's worth it. Make a list, or buy things they've expressed a desire for and save them for special occasions. It's also fun to give a gift when it's not expected.

When your partner considers a gift to be thoughtful, it makes a big impact. When it's given without much care or thought, your partner may think, "You don't really know me," "Did you put any thought into this?" or "This is what you want. It's not what I want." Gift giving is a skill that you can develop. If your partner is a fairly clueless gift-giver, you might need to encourage them and let them know the kinds of things you would genuinely want to receive by saying, "That would make a great gift!" or "I would be really happy if I got that!"

It's quite possible that if you don't regularly express affection for your partner, they may look elsewhere to have their needs met. Be assured that they'd prefer to have their needs met by you, but if you think that saying, "I love you" twice a year on Valentine's Day and their birthday is enough, you may be in for a rude awakening. All of us want and appreciate genuine expressions of love. Tenderly and often, let your partner know how much you care for them.

I knew a man who five days a week would walk by my office carrying flowers on his way home from work. When I asked him why, he replied earnestly, "Because I love my wife." What impressed me was how frequently he bought flowers for her. I'm not saying that bringing flowers needs to be a daily event, but it's a reminder that taking an action that clearly says "I love you" is most welcome, and can rarely be done too often.

As with many things in life, there's an ideal balance. Although there are many people who don't offer enough affection, it's possible to go too far in the other direction. Some people go over the top, say and do too much, and come off as insincere. It can be made worse by poor timing. Be sensitive to overwhelming your partner, and be aware of the appropriate times to communicate your affection.

Saying "I love you" can have a powerful impact. When you express your affection, say it earnestly. Don't say, "I adore you and remember to take out the garbage!" or "I love you, but you're not doing that right and here's what you should do," as this type of mixed message will significantly decrease or negate the impact of what I hope you're trying to convey.

If your words and actions aren't received or responded to in the ways that you would like them to be, have patience. Your partner might not be receptive when you're ready to give, and it may have little or nothing to do with you. At an appropriate time, ask them what's going on for them and what they need. If you're right for each other, everything will work out.

Here are some ways to offer verbal or written expressions of love. Feel free to use them if they reflect what you're willing to sincerely communicate. You might say,

- "When I'm with you, I feel ____."
- "What makes you very special to me is ____."
- "What I appreciate about you is ____."
- "What you do for me that no one else ever has is ____."
- "I'm very fortunate to be with you because ____."
- "I want to share with you a few of the many reasons that I love you."

Be true to yourself, and only say things that you believe reflect what you're thinking and feeling. That said, be willing to move out of your comfort zone so you can keep your communication vibrant. Periodically vary what you do and say, keeping your words and actions loving and respectful. Some people need variety and change. It keeps them interested, excited, and looking forward to what's next. For others, stability and consistency are comforting and make them happy.

When you use terms of endearment, it's wise to reserve most, if not all of them, for your partner. If everyone is your "honey," "sweetie," "baby," or "darling," when you say those words to you partner, you may rob them of the joy of feeling special. As a sign of respect, be sensitive to what you call other people, even when your partner isn't close by.

In a relationship, there may be times when one person is willing to be kind and affectionate, but only if the other person behaves that way first. This often results in an unhealthy standoff. I recommend taking the lead. If you want something, try giving it. If you want generosity, be generous; if you want affection, display affection. If your partner doesn't offer it back in a way that satisfies you, tell them how good you would feel if they were to do what makes you feel appreciated and loved.

Sharing affection with an open heart is one of the greatest gifts we can give to our partner. If we were to lose someone close to us and then magically could once again speak with them, the first thing most of us would say is, "I love you." Sometimes we take for granted the people who are here with us now, and we believe that there's plenty of time to let them know how we feel. Open yourself to both giving and receiving expressions of love, and allow your relationship to flourish.

9

The Gifts of Time and Attention

When you come to the place in your life when you realize that time is precious, you become more selective about how you spend your time and to whom you give your attention. When you give these gifts, it's a way of saying, "What's most valuable to me, I want to share with you."

When you give your time and attention to your partner, they're likely to experience the joy that comes with genuinely feeling cared for. There's no substitute for giving these gifts to another person in a way that makes them feel heard, respected, and honored.

Spending time with another person isn't the same as paying attention to them. We can do one without doing the other, with little impact. However, when the two are combined, the effect is much more powerful than the sum of its parts.

When we get accustomed to being around our partner and know them well, we may begin to tune them out or not give them our full attention, and thus not hear the messages they're trying to convey. Through a combination of familiarity, comfort, and laziness, we may take for granted that they're there, and lose sight of how important they are to us.

When your concentration is elsewhere, your partner's voice may become background noise that you don't notice. You may find yourself agreeing to do something and then have no idea what you agreed to do. If you find yourself regularly saying, "Would you repeat that?" "Excuse me, what did you say?" or the popular "Yes, dear, that's fine," take a closer look at your behavior. You're physically present but aren't listening to the conversation. You may not intentionally be tuning your partner out, but it may seem that way to them. Remember that you chose to be with your partner, and hopefully you feel fortunate to be in a loving relationship with them. Tuning them out will definitely not foster the closeness you want.

It's possible that you're intentionally withholding your full attention. You may be angry with your partner and are trying to "get even." You may believe that you're not getting enough attention, so you respond in kind. You may think that your needs aren't being respected or fulfilled, and possibly you're feeling sadness, shame, and anger. Rather than talking to your partner about how you're feeling, you respond angrily, or by withdrawing in a passive-aggressive manner.

If you're not tuning your partner out on purpose, it's possible that you never developed the ability to completely give your attention to someone else. If this skill doesn't come naturally to you, begin by trying it a few minutes at a time. Do your best to eliminate other distractions and truly focus on your partner. Focused attention is something that many people rarely receive, so it can be a powerful way of connecting. If you find yourself distracted or have difficulty concentrating, it's fine to apologize and ask your partner to repeat something by telling them the last thing you clearly remember. If you add, "What you're saying is very important to me. I want to make sure that I hear and understand you," it will be appreciated.

People usually know whether we're focused on them. If we're aware that we're distracted or troubled by something else, it's worth saying so. Denying or hiding it rarely works. Regardless of our reasons for not giving our partner our full attention, it's important that we try our best to be there for them when they want or need us. While it may be okay to occasionally ask to talk or connect with them at another time, there's usually no time like the present to focus on your partner.

The other day, I was angry about something that was not easy for me to talk about, and I could have continued to act toward my partner in what I recognized to be a passive-aggressive manner. Instead, I talked honestly and openly with her. When I believed that she didn't fully understand what I was trying to convey, I repeated my concerns and spoke my truth using different words. She responded with sensitivity and understanding, and

I felt the joy of being respected and cared for. My anger, sadness, and shame quickly dissipated, and I was able to thank her for genuinely hearing me. This entire process took fifteen minutes. Afterwards I felt even more love for her, and without resentment, I was able to move on to a lighter topic of conversation.

Her gifts of time and attention saved me hours of feeling misunderstood and not as connected to her as I want to be. Had the issue remained unspoken and thus unresolved, it would have had a negative impact on our day. She'd been unaware of my concern until I brought it up, so if we hadn't discussed the issue, unpleasant thoughts and feelings would have festered within me, and she wouldn't have realized why I was distant.

It's surprising and pleasing how quickly someone can feel close to you when they receive your full and undivided attention. Giving undivided attention to your partner overlaps with the third and fourth levels of listening we discussed in the first chapter, "The Art of Listening."

When you regularly give your time and attention to your partner, it's much more likely that you'll receive it from them. However, if you spend time with them without being attentive, it can result in frustration, especially when you think that you're being generous with your time, and they're unsatisfied with what they perceive to be a lack of attention.

When your partner requests that you spend more time with them, it's often because they want more of an emotional connection with you. When you completely focus on them, you may be surprised to find that the connection that they want will come more quickly than you might have thought.

One reason for going to a therapist, coach, or spiritual counselor is that these professionals provide an environment where a person can receive undivided attention. There are usually many other benefits from these interactions, but the gifts of time and attention from the therapist or counselor are built into the dynamic. It feels good to have another person fully focus on your concerns and needs. While I'm not encouraging you to act as your partner's therapist, giving your full and undivided attention to your partner can help fulfill their need to be heard and feel valued.

Just as you can give time without being attentive, you can give attention but not enough time. People can become overwhelmed and distracted with work or with the responsibilities of taking care of children or other relatives. They may spend too much time at work, in front of the television or the computer, with friends, or engaged in hobbies. As a result, it's highly likely that there are too few moments left over to satisfy their partner's need for quality time spent together.

I believe that many affairs start because of an unfulfilled need to be heard and cared for. When you give the gifts of time and attention, you're striving to meet those needs, making it less likely that your partner will look elsewhere for comfort and understanding.

There's no time like the present to fully focus on your partner. Being together allows you to connect in satisfying and pleasurable ways. Do this on a regular basis and you may be surprised to find that you're both very happy. Remember to respect their desire to spend time only with you, being social with others, and by themselves.

Be aware that spending time together rarely resolves issues that are unspoken or ignored. Fortunately, with open, sensitive, and caring communication, you can address these issues. Even if a problem cannot be resolved in the moment, do your best to listen to your partner, and speak your truth. You don't have to be an expert in understanding psychological dynamics, or to be able to solve every problem, for your partner to be content in your relationship.

A strong bond can be formed doing activities that you both take pleasure in, even though they may not necessarily involve focusing directly on each other. Watching movies and television together, as well as going to sporting events and concerts, often connects couples.

Try to find the right balance between concentrating on an event and giving attention directly to each other. Be aware of using activities as a distraction from underlying issues not being voiced by one or both of you. Focus directly on whatever isn't being addressed, or you'll risk an underlying feeling of dissatisfaction. Once you've talked about and hopefully resolved whatever was previously unaddressed, sharing an event or activity together will be much more pleasurable.

Rarely is there a valid reason for not spending enough focused time with each other. If neither of you makes the effort, it will jeopardize the happiness and longevity of your relationship. If either partner is dissatisfied with the amount of time or attention they're getting, it's a problem that should be addressed. Be honest with each other and find a balance so that both of you are happy. Part of the "dance" of a relationship includes meeting each partner's need for quality time and loving attention. I recommend lavishing these gifts on each other.

10

Agreements

To keep your relationship flourishing in a safe and trusting environment, I recommend having agreements that are unambiguous, and that respect and support the relationship that's ideal for both of you. When agreements between partners are honored, love and intimacy can thrive.

WHEN YOU UPHOLD the agreements you make with each other, you establish trust and create a bond that allows you to truly make love, rather than only having sex. Those of you who have experienced the difference know that it's a powerful one. A bond of understanding, commitment, trust, and love allows you to have a wonderful relationship.

Agreements should be clear and verbally agreed to by both parties. It's easy to have misunderstandings that can have significant consequences if the guidelines of your relationship are ambiguous.

If we played a game without any rules, it could quickly spiral out of control. The same can happen in a relationship if one person thinks that there's a clear understanding in place, while the other isn't even aware that one exists. To avoid potential problems, I'm in favor of having agreements that are as unambiguous as possible. Be very specific about your respective definitions of monogamy so that there's a crystal-clear understanding between the two of you. It's one thing to know who takes out the garbage and another thing entirely to be certain about what it means to be faithful to your partner.

Some couples may benefit from writing down their agreements. This may help them avoid arguments that result from misunderstandings. If both of you think that writing them down is a good idea, do it. However, I believe that verbally discussing and agreeing to them is enough.

It's important to talk with each other about the consequences of breaking an agreement. Once agreements are in place, they don't have to be discussed unless one or both of you want to talk about them. If the rules of your relationship are clearly understood and agreed to, both partners should respect and honor them. Agreements aren't open to unilateral change. It isn't okay to break them even if you judge that your partner isn't holding up their end. If you think that a violation of an agreement has occurred, it's important to talk about it and get clarity about what has been said or done.

If you believe that one or more of your agreements is unrealistic or unfair, try renegotiating and finding new common ground, rather than violating an agreement and having to deal with the consequences. The need to apologize and forgive is kept to a minimum when you both live up to your word.

When you uphold your end of your commitments, you can, in turn, expect the same from your partner. If you're faithful, you can expect your partner to be faithful. If you act honestly, you can expect the same. If you model trustworthiness for your partner, they'll understand that you're serious about your commitment to your relationship. You deserve to be with someone who will treat you as well as you treat them. You can set the standard by acting with integrity.

What if you have violated an agreement? My uncle taught me that one important sign of maturity is the willingness to apologize if you've done something wrong. A sincere apology should include not only the words "I'm sorry," but also an acknowledgment of what you're sorry for saying, doing, or in some cases, not saying or doing. When a person only says, "I'm sorry," it's often not clear to me what they're apologizing for. I don't know what the person meant or what they're feeling. When a criminal gets caught and only says, "I'm sorry," I think what they mean is, "I'm sorry that I got caught and I'll be punished."

When apologizing, your words and tone of voice should convey sincerity and an acknowledgment that what you did has hurt the other person and possibly damaged your relationship. I recommend letting your partner know that you understand the impact that your words or actions have had. Communicate a clear intention to do or say things differently, going forward.

An apology should not come with an expectation that it will be immediately accepted. Don't expect that the other person's feelings will or should change on your timeline. Give your partner time to absorb and hopefully accept your genuine and sincere apology.

Some people learn early in life to apologize for things they didn't do, and to take the blame for things that were not their fault. These people will benefit from learning to speak their truth and not to blame themselves as a way to "keep the peace." They will need to navigate the delicate balance between self-blame when it isn't warranted and maturely apologizing when it's appropriate.

It's also important to recognize that you may unknowingly do or say something that has an unintended consequence. You may not have set out with a conscious intent to hurt your partner, but they may be hurt nonetheless. Tell them if your words or actions were genuinely innocent and without bad intent. However, know that regardless of your intent, there's no excuse for ignoring the impact that your words or actions have had. When you take responsibility for your role in what has occurred, it goes a long way toward strengthening your bond.

If one partner violates their agreement to be monogamous, it will take more than an apology to heal the wounds that have been inflicted. It may take the assistance of a trained professional to facilitate your communication, help you understand the dynamics of what has happened, and support and guide you through the healing process, if it's possible to repair the relationship. I'm reminded of the saying, "Trust is broken in waves and regained in drips."

There are some relationships in which couples, over time and with great effort, are able to overcome the wounds caused by infidelity. These couples do the hard work of addressing the underlying reasons for the affair, and then recommit to each other. Months or years later, both partners may agree that the wounds have healed. However, seeing the pain that all parties suffer during the healing process makes me realize how important it is to honor your commitments. When it comes to keeping your relationship happy and thriving, it's worth upholding your agreements, or trying to renegotiate them if you no longer believe that you can honor them. When it comes to potential damage to your relationship, an ounce of prevention is definitely worth a pound of cure.

In the course of a long-term relationship, there are bound to be circumstances when one partner apologizes and the other has the opportunity to accept the apology. Asking for forgiveness isn't easy, and forgiving can be difficult depending on the circumstances. Each partner may consider some actions forgivable and some not.

If you forgive another person, it doesn't have to imply that what they did is acceptable. You don't need to forget it ever happened. It may take a long time before trust is reestablished. Existing agreements may need to be reaffirmed or changed, with both partners being very clear about what the consequences would be if another violation were to occur.

I find it easy to move on from most arguments and misunderstandings. At the same time, I'm less forgiving if agreements that I hold in high regard are violated, including those related to fidelity and honesty. I hold myself to a high standard and expect the same from my partner. Everyone is different, and it's up to each partner to decide which violations are deal breakers and which could more easily be accepted and excused.

Not every relationship will last forever. Even if your relationship is showing signs of stress or is ending, continue to uphold your agreements. Then, if your relationship doesn't work out and you break up, it will be easier to honor what you once had, and to be proud of how you acted. If the relationship does last, it will be a lot easier to reestablish your connection if you have acted honorably. Remember that how your partner acts is a reflection of who they are, and how you act is a reflection of who you are.

Although people can and often do rationalize just about any behavior, remaining true to your word allows you to stay in integrity with yourself. When you can honestly say that you keep your agreements, your next partner will be more likely to trust and believe in you.

I sincerely hope that you're happy, and confident that your partner is the best person with whom to experience a beautiful life. However, if you aren't happy, communicate your unhappiness and give yourselves an opportunity to make things better by addressing your challenges. When you do this, neither of you is likely to break an agreement. Communicating openly and lovingly about issues that may be difficult to discuss is much less painful than dealing with the broken hearts that often accompany broken agreements.

Honor and respect yourself and your partner by doing the right thing, so that your love can grow in an atmosphere of safety and trust.

11

Satisfying Your Partner's Needs

When you do your best to satisfy your partner's needs, you demonstrate that you care about their happiness. When you don't wait for your needs to be met first before trying your best to meet theirs, you show yourself to be a loving partner worthy of acknowledgment and appreciation.

WHEN BOTH PEOPLE in a relationship are happy, it's often because they're enjoying bringing happiness into each other's lives. When you're both able to share what makes you feel cared for and loved, and you strive to fulfill each other's needs, a more intimate emotional and physical connection will follow.

Meeting the needs of your partner starts with a willingness and desire to contribute to their happiness.

Next comes the process of finding out what they want. It can be frustrating when you don't know what brings your partner joy, or when you find that what you used to do to make them happy no longer seems to have the same effect.

Asking your partner what makes them feel good may not sound romantic, but it's an excellent place to start. If you ask, "What can I say or do that would make you feel really good?" they will be pleasantly surprised, because people don't hear that question too often. At first, their response may be that they're already happy, but as they realize that you're serious, they may become more forthcoming. Most of the time they will offer ideas that are reasonable and achievable, and as a result of your willingness to ask and then act, you will show yourself to be a caring and considerate partner.

If the two of you are meant to be together, your partner will not make unreasonable demands of you. They will be sensitive to your ability to please them, and will ask things of you that you're able to do. You can let them know that your intention is for them to be as happy as possible, and you'll do your best to act in ways that demonstrate that fulfilling their needs is important to you.

Be aware that one of the most common and disturbing cycles that can develop in a relationship occurs if both people wait for their needs to be met before they try to meet their partner's needs. It's easy for a person to get caught up in a self-righteous behavior pattern in which they're only willing to put forth love and attention if their partner does it first.

Why does this cycle start? Often it's because one or both people have been wounded emotionally by something their partner has said or done. Sometimes the emotionally hurtful experience goes unmentioned and thus is never discussed. Consciously or not, one or both people take a resentful or angry stand and refuse to give their partner what they want unless their own emotional needs are met first. When this happens, the tension between partners normally increases, resulting in diminished intimacy. After a while, one or both people may forget what they were initially mad about or hurt by, but they'll still respond based on their emotional wound.

The best way to break this destructive cycle is to put aside your need to be right and make the initial attempts to reconnect. Approach your partner with sensitivity and a willingness to take responsibility for your part in creating a problem in your relationship. Ask them if there's anything that you have said or done that has them feeling more distant from you. It can be hard to do this, especially when you think that they're "to blame" for what's happening. When you break the cycle of waiting for the other person to approach first, you distinguish yourself as a sensitive and caring partner. A loving connection can often be reestablished quickly, especially when there's mutual love and respect, and you both genuinely want the relationship to succeed. It will take some effort, but it's worth it.

Both of you may have nonsexual needs that can and should be met by another person or group of people. In fact, you and your partner may be looking to each other for fulfillment that should be gotten elsewhere. If either partner looks to the other to fill all their needs for socializing and emotional connection, it will have a negative impact on the relationship. Friends, support groups, therapists, and coaches can all be part of a support system that can enhance rather than threaten your relationship. Reaching out to others for support should be done with respect for and sensitivity to your partner.

As in most situations, finding the right balance is important. If you're spending too much time with others, your partner may feel ignored. If you spend too little time away from them, they may feel smothered or overwhelmed, and experience the burden of thinking that they alone are responsible for your happiness. When the two of you trust each other, socializing to meet your respective needs shouldn't be a threat. If it feels threatening, it's important to discuss your feelings and do your best to find a balance that will satisfy both of you.

As part of meeting your partner's needs, find out how often they want to be by themselves, spend time alone with you, socialize as a couple, or spend time by themselves with friends or family. Start by asking what's most important to them, and how you can support them in getting what they want.

It's not uncommon for one person to think that they're reasonable, easy to be with, and communicative, while their partner is unreasonable, demanding, and uncommunicative. Be aware of this, as it's quite possible that your partner is reasonable and communicative. The more that you're willing to fulfill their desires without compromising your integrity, the more likely it is that your kindness will be reciprocated. If you were very similar to each other in every way, it might be wonderful for a short time but likely terribly boring soon after, so support them even when their needs are different from yours.

When your partner is telling you how you can fulfill their desires, be aware of your own internal dialogue that might say, "I have not been able to satisfy them and I'm not good enough." Try your best to avoid the all-too-common reaction of believing that because they have needs that aren't completely being met, you haven't been or will never be enough for them. Chances are that you're more than good enough, and now is the time for you to take your relationship to an even greater level of happiness and satisfaction. If you only listen to their requests through a filter of shame, sadness, and fear, you won't hear what they're really asking for. Instead, you will be mired in your own thoughts, which doesn't allow for the highest level of listening that we discussed in "The Art of Listening" chapter.

When your partner tells you what they want and need, listen attentively rather than simultaneously compiling a list of what you want. When you hear their requests and respond with as little judgment as is possible, you encourage them to be more open. If their response to you is "Everything is fine" or "Everything is okay," let them know that you really want things to be more than okay, and you want to make your relationship even better by fulfilling as many of their desires as possible.

Don't assume that you're meeting their needs merely because you're doing or saying what you have always done. A person's desires can change over time. When you ask what you can do to meet their needs, it's as if you're asking your partner for the numbers that open the combination lock to their heart. It's possible that this "secret" has changed over time. Your partner wants you to know what opens their heart, and they will usually be glad to tell you if asked.

Change is the one constant in life. Rather than resist it, try to welcome it. Ask your partner what needs you can help them fill that will keep them feeling great about your relationship. If you can respond before dissatisfaction arises, you'll be more likely to have an appreciative partner who wants to make sure that you're happy, too.

12

How to Get Your Needs Met

You honor yourself by believing that your reasonable needs are important enough to be met. When you effectively communicate your desires to your partner, and then support them in satisfying your needs, it gives both of you an opportunity to be happy and content.

IN THE PREVIOUS chapter we emphasized the importance of satisfying your partner's needs before addressing how your own can be met. This isn't meant to imply that your needs are any less important. Your needs are equally important; however, when you take the initiative and make every effort to bring your partner happiness, there's a much better chance that your needs will also be met. While giving is a reward in itself, your requests will fall on more receptive ears if your partner can tell from your words and actions that your ultimate goal is for you to be as happy together as possible.

If you're reading this book before your partner does, then I hope that you'll do your best to satisfy their desires, even if you judge that they're not making enough of an effort to fulfill yours. If you're the type of person who takes pleasure in receiving as well as giving, you may experience even more satisfaction when your efforts are recognized and returned in kind.

When working with clients, one of the first things that I ask is, "What do you want?" For many people this is a more challenging question to answer than it may seem. Many people are quick to share what they don't want, and express feelings of sadness, anger, and fear that often accompany their dissatisfaction and lack of fulfillment. Unfortunately, too often these people are slow to communicate their needs and desires in a way that would most likely result in greater happiness for them.

Some people hesitate to openly express what they want because there's a part of them that senses that if they express a need and it's fulfilled, they may still be unsatisfied. Asking for what you think will make you happy and then still being unsatisfied when you receive it may reveal deeper truths that are difficult to face. It's possible that what you really want cannot be satisfied by your partner, or perhaps by anyone else.

When you ask, "What do I want from life?" admit to yourself that your partner can help satisfy some of your important desires, but not all of them. When you ask them to fulfill needs that you can and should fulfill yourself, you put an unfair burden on them. You cannot be their best lover, ever, if you're looking to them to be the sole source of your happiness and the only person responsible for your enjoyment of life.

After deciding what you want, distinguish needs that you can meet on your own from those that your partner can join you in satisfying. Rather than putting an unnecessary strain on your partner, you may find that friends, social groups, or professional therapists are more appropriate people to rely on to get certain needs met.

While you're deciding what needs could be satisfied on your own, don't minimize, suppress, or keep hidden from your partner what makes you genuinely happy, and what can help to maintain the strong bond between you. One or both of you may have unexpressed desires that if not met, can jeopardize the health of your relationship. When you do ask your partner to help you fulfill your needs, communicate sensitively and respectfully, especially if you want them to embrace being a part of making you happy. I hope that they won't be flippant about or belittle your requests. If they do, you're probably not in the right relationship.

Of the needs that can be met by or with your partner, decide which are most important to you. Approaching your partner with many requests at once may overwhelm them. If they don't know where to start, or if they think that no matter what they do it won't be enough, they're much less likely to be receptive. To increase the likelihood of your needs being met, start by expressing one or two desires that are important to you, rather than presenting a laundry list of demands.

When you're ready to approach your partner, do it at an appropriate time. Examples of some inappropriate times include during or immediately after an argument, in the middle of a crucial task, as one of you is just coming in or running out the door, or during other hurried moments.

If you're ready to talk and you believe that your timing is appropriate, but it never seems to be the right time for your partner, stress that what you have to say is important. Ask for enough time to be set aside so you can talk, be heard, and further discuss whatever you'll be bringing up.

When you have found an appropriate time, don't imply or say, "This is what I want. Figure out a way to make it happen." Let your partner know that you're ready to work with them to satisfy your needs and theirs.

Even if you're being reasonable and appropriate when you ask for what you want, you may face hesitation, resistance, or a response from your partner that reflects their fear, sadness, and shame. As mentioned previously, rather than hearing what's being said, some people may turn their partner's requests into a reflection of their self-perceived inadequacy.

To maximize the possibility of getting what you want, it's important to communicate effectively. How you ask for what you want matters. While being polite and respectful should be a given, the two of you may have different personalities and ways of expressing yourselves.

Since your partner is likely more receptive to a specific communication style, understanding your partner's personality can make a big difference in determining how favorably your request will be received.

If your partner has an amiable personality type, they may be very willing to fulfill requests when asked nicely and respectfully, but they may become resistant and less communicative when they're told to do something. When people with predominantly amiable personalities are told what to do, they may not verbally express their unhappiness, but they may react in a passive-aggressive manner by withholding their affections, by not fulfilling requests, or by shutting down and withdrawing. Amiable personality types are people-oriented and enjoy the closeness of partnership, family, and friends. You're more likely to get what you want if they're appreciated and thanked for their efforts.

If your partner has an analytical personality type, they also want to be asked rather than told what to do. If you tell your analytical partner what you want done, be prepared to meet resistance, which they may not express verbally. People with analytical personalities are task-oriented. They're also detail-oriented and may ask a lot of questions that will better allow them to "analyze and solve a problem." They enjoy being thought of as experts, so ask for their ideas about how to best accomplish what you're proposing. You're more likely to get what you want if a plan is made and agreed to that involves specific, measurable, and achievable goals.

If your partner has a driven personality type, they will respond well when presented with the opportunity to accomplish a task or tasks in order to achieve a goal. They can more easily be told what to do, and can be approached with, or asked for, a specific plan to fulfill your desires. It's best to be direct in your communication rather than "wasting their time" by not being forthright. When approached in the correct way, they're very good at taking action and "getting things done," so fulfilling a specific need can become something to be accomplished. You're more likely to get what you want if they devise a plan that lets them know that they're important and in charge of "fixing the problem and achieving the goal." The problem can be that some of your needs aren't being met, and the goal is to meet those needs.

If your partner has an expressive personality type, they're people-oriented. Unlike amiable and analytical personality types, they can more easily be told what to do. Help them feel respected and special by giving them lots of time to talk openly and excitedly. If they seem to be too long-winded, you can interrupt them, but only if you quickly move on to another topic of conversation. They're often very friendly and bubbly, but become unhappy and assertive when they don't get their way. People with expressive personalities get bored easily and rarely hide their emotions, so it's best to keep your communication lively and interesting. You're more likely to get your needs met if your needs can be satisfied in ways that are fun, fast-paced, and exciting.

Many people are a mix of personality types and they may act differently in their relationships than in other areas of their lives. I recommend paying attention to whether your partner seems to be responding favorably to your requests and suggestions. If you're not getting the responses that you want, before giving up, try varying your style of communication. The words that you use and how you communicate with your partner are very important when it comes to getting what you desire.

You may find that you have needs that can only be met as your relationship develops and matures, and you trust each other more. When you give your relationship time to evolve, and you respect each other's abilities and limitations, you'll find that your desires have a higher likelihood of being met. It's unrealistic to expect that all of your needs will be fulfilled, but as you communicate effectively and make efforts to satisfy your partner's desires, hopefully you will get more of what you want.

If you have needs that aren't currently being met but were met in the early stages of your relationship, there's a great possibility that they once again can be satisfied. There's often a passion that marks the initial months of courtship. Although many things between you get better with time, the initial intensity and fire may have waned. Before asking your partner to act as they once did, you can ask yourself, "How did I show up in the early stages of our relationship that's different from how I'm acting now? How might I be responsible for the diminished intensity, and how can I contribute to recapturing some of our initial passion?" Admit how your behavior may have changed over time, and be willing to act as you once did in order hopefully to reignite those initial flames of passion. When you share your desire for what you experienced earlier in the relationship, be willing to do your part. Your efforts may very well be appreciated and matched.

It's quite possible that what you currently want doesn't involve passion and romance. Your desires may be more "practical" and involve the experiences and routines of daily living, such as sharing responsibilities more equitably, spending more time together, or talking more about how your day has been. I hope that you will express what you want, generate ideas to get those needs met, and find your partner to be receptive and understanding. For some people, getting seemingly simple desires met opens their hearts in a way that allows for intimacy to flourish.

The art of compromise comes into play when you talk about how to meet each other's needs. Compromise should not be about one of you winning and the other losing; instead, it should be about both of you ending up as happy as possible. Whether or not all of your needs are satisfied, you will benefit greatly from getting clarity about what you want, and then respectfully expressing your desires. Ultimately, both of you will learn more about yourselves and your relationship.

It's important to examine whether we are making unreasonable demands of our partners. We may have areas of our lives that are unsatisfying, and we may look to our partner to take responsibility for our unpleasant feelings. Being in a committed, monogamous relationship should come with many satisfying benefits; however, tension can result from making unreasonable requests.

Our partners should complement our lives and in some ways complete us, but it's important to realize that we are ultimately responsible for our own happiness.

Certain needs, of course, should only be met within our relationship, including our desires for sexual and nonsexual physical intimacy. There are other needs that are also reasonable for us to expect our partner to meet. However, if your desires seem unreasonable to them, you will have to decide whether to stay in your relationship, or search for another person with whom you think you can be happier.

Before moving on, which may be a drastic and unnecessary change, examine whether your dissatisfaction seems to follow a pattern from one relationship to another. We often repeat the same mistakes until we learn certain lessons, and it may be the case that you'll end this relationship only to then attract similar partners and circumstances into your life.

I also suggest exploring what feelings you hope to experience once one or more of your seemingly important needs are met. Pleasure can take a variety of different forms. Think about what you genuinely want as a result of a specific request. Do you want pleasure that comes from thinking that your partner believes that you're attractive, sexy, intelligent, and clever? Do you want happiness that comes from thinking that you're desired, or that your talents and gifts are appreciated? Do you want reassurance, a feeling of safety, or the joy of connection with your partner? This could be a long list, and I recommend that you create your own. Once you have more clarity about what you truly want, use your insight and intelligence to better communicate your genuine needs and how they could be met.

As an example of a request that doesn't reflect what someone really wants, let's say that a person asks their partner to contact them every hour to tell them what they're doing. After going through the process of uncovering what they really want, the person may discover that they want to feel the joy that comes from hearing that they're loved, desired, and often thought about.

If they asked their partner to say to them, "I love you and you're very important to me. I think about you often throughout the day. I'm excited about seeing you tonight," and their partner willingly filled their request, their underlying needs would quite likely be met, and their impractical request for contact every hour would be unnecessary. When you uncover what you want and then make requests in a straightforward and kind way, you'll be much more likely to get your real needs fulfilled.

It's possible that one or both of you are among a large group of people who struggle to believe that they're as important as other people. If your partner is among this group, when they express that they're deserving of having their needs fulfilled, it's a personal breakthrough. Respect your partner for asking for what they want, and if you're not asking for what you want, demonstrate that same courage. Remember that asking that your desires be considered important is a far cry from being needy.

Distinguish reasonable requests that can be met within your relationship from an unhealthy desire to have your partner take responsibility for your happiness. Then, communicate what you want in a loving way so that your partner can really hear you. You're likely to find yourself much happier as more of your needs are fulfilled.

13

Nonsexual Physical Intimacy

Nonsexual physical intimacy is an essential part of a healthy relationship. Touching your partner with warmth and tenderness can convey the depth of your affection. For many people, receiving their partner's love though nonsexual intimate gestures is more important to them than having sex.

NONSEXUAL PHYSICAL INTIMACY is one of the great pleasures that we can experience in life. If you're fortunate to be with a partner you love, I encourage you to reach out to them frequently with a warm and caring touch. Too many people in a committed relationship yearn for more intimate displays of their partner's love. When you share physical affection in genuinely loving, nonsexual ways, it helps validate for your partner how much they mean to you.

Nonsexual intimate gestures include hugging, kissing, touching, holding hands, massage, cuddling, and any other loving physical contact between you that doesn't include having sex or the expectation of having sex. I recommend frequently using nonsexual intimate gestures as an expression of your affection for your partner, rather than reserving them only for when you're interested in having sex. Although it's possible that displaying your affection in these ways may lead one or both of you to have a heightened interest in sex, this should not be your motivation.

It goes without saying that there are different types of love. You can love your family, friends, and pets, but nothing compares to the unique feeling of being in love with your partner, and experiencing the delight of interacting in ways meant only for the two of you.

I believe that all physical intimacy should only be between you and your partner. Therefore, in my opinion, any type of physical intimacy between you and someone other than your partner breaks the agreement you have regarding being monogamous. This doesn't, of course, preclude you from hugging another person as an expression of caring and friendship.

There are people for whom hugging and holding hands come easily, and they don't ascribe much or any important meaning to these gestures. People who are naturally very physically expressive should be sensitive to how their actions may be interpreted by other people. They should be respectful of their partner and of whomever they're hugging or being affectionate with, and realize that others may possibly misinterpret their actions.

An important factor in these types of gestures is a person's intent. People you interact with can usually tell if your intentions are honorable. Be sensitive about giving the wrong impression, and if you believe that a physical gesture you made has been or could be misinterpreted, clear it up as soon as possible. Also, if you believe that someone isn't acting honorably, you should establish healthy boundaries with that person.

Touch is a basic human need. People's preferences as to how much and how often they want to be touched vary, but I believe that most people have a desire to be touched more frequently. Touch your partner in the ways and with a frequency that makes them happy, or they may consider going to someone else in order to meet this vital need. If you don't feel comfortable communicating through touch, it's time to practice! Get feedback from your partner as to what feels good to them, and if necessary, ask when and how often they enjoy being touched.

Along with giving more physical expressions of affection, I encourage you to ask respectfully for what you want, whether it's more hugs, kisses, massages, or any other kinds of nonsexual physical closeness. Allowing each other to say, "I want a hug," "I want a kiss," or "Please hold me," and then giving this gift, can be a beautiful expression of intimacy.

Close physical contact should be well timed so that your touches are associated with a loving connection between you. If your hugs or kisses are given only when tension between you is high, your partner may get mixed and confusing associations with your touch. If you only offer nonsexual physical gestures after an argument, it may lead your partner to believe that they can only get their need for physical closeness met by arguing with you. Conversely, if you touch each other when you're both happy and relaxed, your touches are much more likely to be associated with something pleasurable.

Sadly, many people's childhood environment didn't afford them the opportunity to give or receive much appropriate and caring physical contact. Just as the ability to say "I love you" is influenced by how often you heard this from a loving parent or caretaker, a person's ability and willingness to express and receive nonsexual affection is influenced by childhood experiences. If either or both of you came from a less expressive background, or haven't experienced many caring or loving relationships, nonsexual touch may be an even more powerful and connecting experience than having sex. It's important for both of you to be sensitive to and understanding of each other's life experiences, while also remembering your own needs.

One challenge that a new relationship may face occurs when people have sex shortly after they meet. The couple may then find themselves making efforts to get their nonsexual and emotional intimacy to catch up to the sexual openness they have already shared. When sex precedes emotional intimacy, behaviors such as holding hands or hugging may at first seem strange or awkward to a new couple. That's one of the reasons some people may "take their time" and want to feel close to someone before being sexually intimate. When two people start to feel genuine affection for each other, nonsexual physical intimacy can be a sweet way of demonstrating their emotions.

For those of you who love animals, be aware that some people are very affectionate with their pet(s) but may neglect the needs of their partner. I have known people who got a pet after their relationship was established and then reduced their physical affection toward their partner. Their attention was divided while they enjoyed "unconditional love" from their pet.

I have seen a similar dynamic apply when a newborn or toddler gets almost all of a parent's attention. While it's perfectly understandable that babies and children need a lot of attention, care, and love, neglecting the needs of your partner will have significant consequences for your relationship. If your desire is to keep your partner happy, express your fondness for them verbally and physically with a frequency that has them feeling appreciated and satisfied.

Just as there doesn't need to be a reason to give a gift, there's no reason needed for giving nonsexual affection. Physical expressions of tenderness and care, when given without a reason, are sweet expressions of love. If you express your affection often enough, your partner's first thought when you touch them won't be, "I wonder what they did that for?" or "I wonder what they want?" Your gestures should be frequent enough that they think or say, "My partner satisfies my needs. I know that they sincerely love me, and they don't touch me only when they want something."

Nonsexual physical intimacy sometimes becomes a prelude to sexual intimacy. Although your intent should only be to express your affection, it's possible that an intimate hug in the morning will make your partner eager to see you, hear your voice, and feel your touch as soon as you're once again in each other's presence.

As long as both of you are satisfied and content, there's no need to make any changes to your relationship. However, too many people don't show enough affection to their partner, and one or both people may become discouraged and give up trying to get their needs met. It's better to give too much than too little, until you find the right balance for both of you. Be generous with your hugs, kisses, smiles, and loving touch, and be sensitive to your partner's responses. Giving and accepting affection without any preconditions or expectations is a beautiful expression of your love for each other.

14

Sexual Intimacy

For committed, monogamous partners, sex can be a beautiful expression of their deep affection and love for each other. Making love can also be playful, joyful, and wonderfully connecting. Satisfying each other's desires is an important part of keeping a relationship exciting.

WHEN PEOPLE SEE a book called *The Best Lover, Ever*, some of them think that it's only about sex. Yet this is the first time that we're discussing the importance of a satisfying sex life. Although it takes a lot more than great sex to be your partner's best lover, ever, for most people it's still an important part of their relationship.

Sexual intimacy with someone you love can be one of the most glorious experiences in life. Since this book is written for those who have chosen to be in a monogamous relationship, my focus will be on making love only with your partner, with the hope and expectation that your sex life will be forever pleasurable. Since sex can be such an intimate, bonding, and wonderful experience, it's very important to make time to enjoy each other.

A great sex life is whatever makes you both happy. There are some couples for whom hugging, kissing, and cuddling is their sex life and they're very content. Some couples make love frequently, yet for one or both people, it never seems like enough. Some couples seem to find the right balance. If you're both genuinely content, wonderful!

That said, please don't make the mistake of thinking that everything is fine simply because *you're* satisfied. Also, don't convince yourself that everything is okay if your partner seems content but you're not. Dissatisfaction with your sex life can be a primary cause of tension and unhappiness. This unhappiness can undermine the foundation of your relationship when either your desires or your partner's go unmet.

Talking with each other about your love life is definitely important, yet for some people it's a difficult subject of conversation because they may associate sex with feelings of fear, sadness, anger, shame, and guilt. I believe that our culture can be immature, puritanical, and fearful when it comes to discussions about sex. Too many people become adults without having enough basic knowledge about the pleasures and consequences of physical intimacy. Many people are unwilling or afraid to talk about what they want. I encourage you to talk openly and respectfully to each other, even at the risk of making one or both of you uncomfortable. You're much more likely to get what you want through honest and loving communication than by ignoring your needs, making demands, or delivering ultimatums.

Be honest about how high a value you put on your sex life, and assume that it's important to your partner, unless they truthfully say otherwise. If neither of you thinks it's important, then you can move it down your list of shared values, as long as you both realize that for one or both of you, your level of interest may change over time. If your own desire has decreased, determine if your overall interest in sex has diminished, or whether it's an issue related to a problem with your relationship.

If you choose to watch pornography, it's important to realize that watching others rarely gives a realistic picture of a healthy sex life, or shows anything close to the real affection and caring that come with genuinely making love. Don't have unrealistic expectations of your partner or yourself based on what's staged and edited, and clearly lacks genuine intimacy.

Before, during, or after making love, tell each other what feels good and what feels great. It's important to be aware of what stimulates and excites both of you. When you're sensitive to your partner's responses while being intimate, you can often determine what they like or love, and what they may not care for as much. Everyone is different, so experiment and ask.

If you've had previous partners, don't assume that your current partner is the same as them. Listen and be open to accepting and giving feedback. Communicate truthfully but gently, for when it comes to sex, one or both of you may be more vulnerable than either of you realizes. Sex can be a delicate topic of conversation, and many people are sensitive as a result of their self-perceived inadequacies.

Let your partner know the many ways in which they're wonderful when it comes to making love. When you honestly tell your partner what they do better than anyone else, you will inspire them to be more open and intimate with you.

What kind of lover are you? Some people are more adventurous than others. Let your partner know how willing you are to be adventurous, and experiment with different ways of having fun between the two of you. For some people, variety is the spice of life and contributes to sexual satisfaction. Be respectful of your partner not wanting to do something, and consider introducing your ideas and desires at a pace that increases the chance that your partner will be open to doing what brings you pleasure.

When speaking intimately during sex, draw a distinction between fantasy and reality. There are many things that one or both of you may enjoy talking about that if explored in reality, would not be good for either of you or for your relationship. When you have a clear understanding that fantasy talk is exclusively for enhancing your sex life, it opens another door to exploring your adventurous spirit. When you're open to discovering what gets both of you excited, you become a better lover.

When making love, some people get more enjoyment from giving than receiving, as giving comes more naturally to them. If you believe that it's good to give but selfish to ask for and receive pleasure, you can change this limiting belief. Use your lovemaking as a vehicle for learning that it's healthy and satisfying to give and receive in all aspects of your life. When you achieve more of a balance between giving and receiving, your sex life will get even better for both of you.

What can you do when one person wants more frequency or variety? While it's unusual for both people to always have their needs met, this is an area of your relationship where you can definitely compromise, while still living with integrity. If you're fortunate to have a partner who gently and directly communicates their desires, try to meet their needs while honoring yourself. If there are emotional issues that are preventing one or both of you from opening yourselves to each other, it's worth addressing these issues. When emotional issues are taken seriously, people are often more willing to open their hearts, which leads to greater intimacy.

One person or both may withhold their affections because they're not feeling good about how they look. They make the mistake of thinking that because they're not attractive to themselves, they're not attractive to their partner. Regardless of how you feel about yourself, it's important to know that when you're making love with your partner, they consider you to be the most attractive person in the world. Don't make the mistake of believing that until you look or feel a certain way, you should withhold your affections. In fact, it's the withdrawal of affection that most often creates sexual dissatisfaction and a distance between partners. Do your best to feel attractive, and remember that we're all unique and beautiful.

What people consider to be a satisfying sex life can vary greatly. I'm reminded of the man in his nineties who said that he and his partner had sex almost every night. He said, "On Monday we almost had it, on Tuesday we almost had it, on Wednesday we almost had it..." If your conversation too often sounds like, "Not today. Maybe tomorrow, or on the weekend," remember that too many empty promises will have a negative effect on your relationship.

Another example of varying perspectives is when a couple makes love once a week and one partner says, "We almost never have sex," while the other partner says, "Whenever we finally get a chance to relax, all they want to do is have sex." While there's no right or wrong, it's important to be aware of and respect your needs and theirs, and do your best to keep both of you content. Remember that the goal is to be your partner's best lover, ever. Discovering what makes and keeps them happy increases the chances of them wanting to be with you and only you.

In reality, once a relationship is established, the frequency of physical intimacy often decreases, and the day-to-day routines of life take precedence. If this happens, it's important to make sure that both of you continue to be content. If necessary, set aside time to be intimate, as for most people, sex is still high on the list of what's important to them. Don't always leave sexual intimacy for the end of the day, when you're likely to find yourselves tired, and making love may seem like another chore.

If sex isn't pleasurable or frequent enough, it sets the stage for one or both of you, depending on your personality, to express your sadness or anger, project your feelings onto something else in your relationship, become less communicative and more distant, or pretend that everything's okay when it's not. Dissatisfaction with your sex life may set the stage for wandering eyes and thoughts about cheating or ending a relationship. Often I hear a person say, "I thought I had more time to fix this problem, or at least to pay more attention to it."

There's an expression that when sex between partners is a problem, it becomes ninety percent of what's important in their relationship, and when it's not a problem, it becomes ten percent of what's important. While honoring yourself, make the effort so its importance never becomes anywhere close to ninety percent. Just as you work on other aspects of your relationship, you may need to pay more attention to your sex life, and it's well worth the effort!

As a lover, be self-confident while not boasting about your talents or asking for constant validation. While it's good to be confident in your abilities, remember that sex isn't the only thing that keeps a relationship thriving. When it comes to your partner's overall happiness, don't delude yourself into thinking that your lovemaking abilities alone are enough to keep your partner content. Only in the context of a great relationship will your lovemaking abilities truly be appreciated.

Being sexually intimate with your partner is a wonderful way to express your love. Support and encourage each other to be open about what makes your sex life satisfying, and do your best to meet each other's desires.

15

Acceptance

When you free yourself from harsh judgments and unrealistic expectations of your partner, your communication becomes more loving, and the bond between you is strengthened. When you embrace your partner as they are, your emotional intimacy will deepen.

MANY PEOPLE SAY that what they want more than anything else is a partner who lets them be themselves. "They love me just the way I am" is an expression I hear when someone is saying that all of their idiosyncrasies and choices are welcomed. If you accept a loving, non-abusive partner as they are, you'll find them more relaxed and happy in your presence.

It's likely that both of you have behaviors and habits that annoy each other. It's also possible that neither of you will ever change those behaviors. One definition of love is the willingness to accept another for who they are, whether or not they ever change. Accepting a person as they are doesn't mean that you're happy with everything they say or do. It also doesn't preclude telling your partner how you feel and what you want, and how their words, actions, or inaction affect you.

One thing I often say to my clients is, "People rarely change, and it's even more rare that they change on your timetable." If you're waiting for another person to alter their basic nature, you may be waiting a long time and possibly forever. If change does occur, it will ultimately be due to their motivators, which may have little to do with you.

Conceding that our partner will probably not change, or that if they do, it will rarely happen on our timetable, can bring an inner calm that will make it easier to love them as they are, instead of who we'd like them to be. It can be liberating to recognize that the only aspect of a relationship that we have control over is our own behavior.

Accepting your partner as they are doesn't mean that you need to comply passively with whatever your partner says and does. There's a difference between accepting and acquiescing. Acquiescing means tolerating reluctantly without protesting, and giving in to what someone else wants. Acquiescing often includes devaluing your own importance and ignoring your needs and desires. Acceptance doesn't include giving in or giving up. Acceptance does include evaluating the reality of your current situation, acknowledging that things may never change, and doing what's best for you.

If your partner is abusing drugs, alcohol, or other substances, and is unable to stop, it's likely that they have an addiction. Regardless of their words or actions, it's important to acknowledge that addiction is a disease. While accepting that your partner can only change if they're willing to, encourage them to get help. Despite their genuine love for you and promises that they may make to change, consider counseling for yourself. Speaking with an objective third party will help support you in making the best decision for yourself.

When a person has an addiction, the dependence on a substance can be so powerful that despite their love for you, and despite the serious consequences they'll likely suffer, the addict's drug of choice can become more important than anything else in their lives. This is one of the sad realities of addiction. You cannot make another person want to get better. Don't believe that if you love someone enough, they'll change. If your partner says, "Take me as I am or it means you don't love me," you can let them know that although you may accept and love them, you need to do what's best for yourself and your family.

What's never acceptable is for your partner to threaten or harm you or anyone else. If you decide to stay with someone who's emotionally or physically abusive, do it with your eyes wide open. Don't convince yourself that they will change. Take action to distance yourself from any abusive person. When you don't act to protect yourself, you're acquiescing to and perpetuating your partner's actions. Accept that you're in an unhealthy and potentially dangerous relationship, and protect yourself and your loved ones.

In a non-abusive relationship, a healthy expression of acceptance includes recognizing and acknowledging your partner's strengths and weaknesses. It includes being realistic and honest about your level of happiness. Don't ask or expect another person to be someone who they're not, could never be, or don't want to be. Try to embrace your partner as they are, rather than constantly seeing them through a lens of how you would prefer them to be. Of course, accepting your partner as they are doesn't preclude you from speaking your truth and making decisions that support what's best for you.

Accepting the present as it is while desiring change may seem like an oxymoron, but the two can coexist quite peacefully. When you accept each other as you currently are, while at the same time requesting the changes that you want, you free yourselves to love each other more fully. From this place, you can better decide whether your current partner is the best person for you to enjoy life with.

You may find that some friends and relatives aren't accepting of your relationship. If people want to judge you or your relationship, let them. What matters most is the bond between you and your partner. If you love and cherish each other, no amount of pressure from others can cause you to break up, regardless of the difficulties that their opinions may present.

All of us have a natural tendency to judge. Some people judge others harshly while being gentle when judging themselves. Some people are gentle in their judgment of others while being harsh in their judgment of themselves, and some people are harsh judges of both themselves and others. If you're a harsh judge of your partner and have difficulty accepting them as they are, try an experiment: for one day, listen to and truly hear what they're saying, while doing your best not to judge them. See what happens. When you don't judge your partner, you may find that there isn't anything to fix, and no need to criticize or blame them. Whether or not the experiment seems to go well, try it again the next day, and the day after. Acting in this way gives your partner the gift of feeling the joy of acceptance, and frees you from the burden of having to change or control them.

By allowing a non-abusive, well-intentioned partner to be who they are, you're likely to find that it's much easier and more enjoyable to be together. Accepting your partner as they are lets them experience the joy that comes with knowing that in your eyes they're more than good enough.

16

Appreciation

When your partner feels valued and cared for, they're much more likely to open their heart to you. Letting them know how much you appreciate and love them strengthens the emotional bond that's crucial to a healthy, long-lasting relationship.

WHEN YOUR PARTNER knows how important they are to you, it creates a deep, loving connection that makes it easier to navigate the challenges that are a part of any relationship. Through your words, behaviors, and actions, you have the opportunity to let your partner know how much you appreciate having them in your life. When your thoughtfulness and kindness is returned, you will know that you have found a special person to be with.

Express your admiration for your partner's fine qualities in private and, when appropriate, in front of others.

Most people experience joy when hearing nice things said about them. Actively contribute to your partner feeling valued by respecting their opinions, acknowledging their intelligence, appreciating their sense of humor, and talking about any other special qualities you believe that they have.

Most people don't get enough acknowledgment for the good things they do. Give your partner the recognition they deserve by letting them know how capable, talented, and awesome they are, and how happy you are to be their partner. If their response is, "You're only saying all these nice things because you love me," you can tell them that you do love them and that you're speaking the truth.

One way to demonstrate how much you appreciate your partner is to show respect for what they enjoy doing. Accompany your partner in activities they get pleasure from, with a sincere intention and willingness to enjoy yourself. When there's a healthy balance in your relationship, you will take pleasure in doing this for each other.

If you seem to be taking your partner for granted, you can begin to change this by recognizing and sharing how much you care for them and your relationship. You could say, "You're so important to me. I want to tell you what makes you and our relationship very special," and go into as much detail as you're comfortable with. Letting your partner know how important they are to you isn't something you should do only on Valentine's Day and your anniversary.

When expressing your love and appreciation, it's usually best to do it in a serious manner, as intimate thoughts and feelings may make one or both of you feel vulnerable. My hope is that you'll express yourself honestly and sincerely, and your words will be acknowledged with kindness and love.

Ask yourself if there's anything you could be doing that may be giving your partner the impression that they're not important to you. While this is by no means a comprehensive list, here are some of the things that might make them question how much you appreciate them: not listening, acknowledging, or responding to what they're saying; ignoring their wishes; violating an agreement; acting crudely; being disrespectful, belittling, or insulting to them or their family members; and flirting with other people. I think you get the idea. With relatively little effort you can express and show how much you value and respect your partner, or you can just as easily give the opposite impression.

It's also possible that you may say or do something with the intent of demonstrating how much you appreciate your partner, but the message doesn't get through. One of the best ways to find out if something you have said or done makes someone feel valued is to ask them. Remember that in most successful relationships, people don't expect each other to be mind readers. You could ask, "Did my words and actions show you how much I appreciate you and our relationship?" If your partner's response is less than enthusiastic, ask them, "What are some things that I could do or say that would let you know how special you are to me?"

Another way to show how much you appreciate your partner is by listening to what they want, and doing your best to fulfill their desires. When you demonstrate your willingness to satisfy their needs, it's a way of letting them know how important they are to you.

Although you're not ultimately responsible for what your partner thinks and feels, you can significantly contribute to their overall happiness. Outside of your relationship, your partner may have experiences in which they're unappreciated or devalued. You can boost your partner's self-esteem and lift their spirits by frequently expressing to them how valuable they are to you. When people feel valued, they flourish, and are inspired to contribute to other people's happiness.

In previous chapters we addressed some specific ways that you can demonstrate your respect for your partner and how much they mean to you. One way is to listen attentively when they speak, without trying to fix or correct anything. When you respect their skills and talents, and don't push aside their opinions and impose your own solutions to challenges that they face, you honor them and show that you value their intelligence and problem-solving abilities.

When your partner is truly heard and responded to with care and love, it helps them experience the joy that comes with being valued. Through your words and actions, I encourage you to do what it takes to let your partner know how much you appreciate them.

17

What Makes a Relationship Great?

You're deserving of a wonderful person with whom to share this amazing life. If you have found that special partner and are happy, you're indeed fortunate. Hopefully, your lives are enriched by each other's presence, and you believe that your relationship is well worth the time and energy it takes to keep it thriving.

FOR MOST PEOPLE, being in a committed, monogamous relationship that brings them happiness is high on their list of what's important to them in life. Across the spectrum of what couples value in a relationship, sexual chemistry is very high on some couples' list, while some are perfectly content with nonsexual physical intimacy. Some couples want to do almost everything together, while others prefer more time apart. Some want to know all the details of each other's lives, and some are happy simply knowing that both people are content, faithful, and committed to each other.

What makes a relationship great is different for every couple, and if the two of you feel that what you have is wonderful, that's fantastic! There may still be an idea or two in this book that serves you.

In my discussions with couples that have been together happily for many years, certain values are consistently mentioned as important parts of a strong and devoted relationship. Trust is high on the list. Devoted couples feel that they can trust and count on each other to be there through the best times and the most challenging times. Partners with a strong bond support each other in any way that they can. It may sound trite, but most partners take very seriously their commitment to love, honor, and cherish each other.

Many people consider laughter to be high on the list of what makes their connection special. Couples I interviewed said that enjoying each other's sense of humor, making each other laugh, sharing inside jokes, and seeing the world through a humorous lens are important parts of their relationship.

Having similar ways of looking at life can connect a couple and help to cement their love. Enjoying seemingly simple activities together such as taking walks, sharing meals, listening to music, watching television, and going to concerts, movies, and sporting events, often bonds couples and reminds them of how much they love and enjoy their life.

Shared interests are an important part of a great relationship. A friend of mine is starting over and is hoping for long-term happiness. She's in the initial phase of a new romance and talks excitedly about the things that she and her partner have in common. While romance, passion, and sex can initially keep people attracted to each other, it's genuine love, mutual interests, and ways of enjoying and sharing life together that support a lasting bond.

One hallmark of a wonderful connection is the comfort that comes from feeling safe. Feeling safe and secure takes many forms, and includes freedom from emotional abuse and physical harm. No great relationship can include threats, ultimatums, abuse, or a sense that if you do something that displeases the other person, you will be emotionally or physically attacked. If your partner is emotionally or physically abusive, it's time to give up hope of having a healthy relationship with them. Distance yourself from an abusive partner, end the relationship, get whatever support you need, and when the time is right, find a new partner who's deserving of you.

Mutual respect is a must for any relationship to be successful. Hopefully, your partner brings out your best qualities, has faith in you and your abilities, and encourages and supports you. A great relationship includes expressing gratitude and appreciation for each other's contributions and sacrifices, acknowledging how fortunate you are to be together, and regularly checking in with each other to see if there's any part of your relationship that needs attention.

A devoted relationship includes supporting each other and growing together. A friend said to me, "When I'm troubled, my partner is there and holds me. We give each other room to grow, for the sake of growth in the relationship. If we feel threatened by change, we talk about it and express our feelings."

A close bond includes the ability to forgive. I'm not talking about the ability to forgive an affair or other serious violation of your commitment to each other. Hopefully, such situations will not arise, but if they do, they would call for a deeper act of forgiveness than I'm referring to here. What I'm talking about is the willingness to forgive times when your partner may act selfishly, insensitively, thoughtlessly, or when they're just in a bad mood. I'm not encouraging long-term acceptance of unpleasant behaviors, but rather a willingness to be sensitive to your partner's personal challenges. When sharing your thoughts and feelings with them about their moods and behavior, be honest, gentle, and loving.

Too frequently, people focus on what they judge to be the deficiencies of their partner, pointing out their weaknesses rather than talking about their strengths. I recommend focusing on and acknowledging your partner's many fine qualities, and then singing the praises of your partner, as a way to build and support a great relationship.

The routines and challenges of everyday life sometimes result in a couple taking each other for granted, and they may forget to acknowledge and demonstrate their love for each other. Hopefully, recognizing this possibility reminds them to appreciate the great times they've shared, and to regularly express their affection. Creating and enjoying special times together allows a couple to experience the joy of being in each other's company when they're both relaxed and happy, and reminds them of their love for each other.

I knew a person who was consumed by their professional life, and was often exhausted and not emotionally available when they came home after a long workday. As a result, the couple didn't spend enough time enjoying each other's company. When the hard-working partner was ready to relax and take a vacation, they often did so alone or with another family member. The hard-working partner showed their fun and loving side when they were vacationing, but since the enjoyable times were not shared, a distance grew between the partners. If one person in a relationship is emotionally available, relaxed, open, and loving only at certain times, it becomes even more important that those times be shared.

Some couples in successful relationships have weathered infidelity and worked things out, and they don't regret having made the decision to do the hard work to heal their relationship. Some of these couples say that the reason they stayed together during the very difficult time after the infidelity was first disclosed was for the sake of their children. While having children together may not be the sole reason that people successfully navigate rough waters, it often convinces them to work harder to recapture what they once had. Economic necessity may also keep a couple together long enough to recapture special times and loving feelings. However, financial necessity, shared parenting, or the most expensive jewelry in the world will not keep couples together if they don't work hard to heal wounds and do their best to keep the relationship strong.

When couples have built their relationship on a foundation of love, they will be better equipped to reestablish a trusting connection. If it's useful and when it's appropriate, they can renew their agreements to include doing what it takes to stay fully committed to the health and happiness of their relationship.

Some people hope that their partner will change, while others hope that their partner never will. It's unrealistic to think that your partner will become an idealized version of your perfect mate, or to think that they won't age and thus will always stay as they are. If you can accept them as they are while supporting but not demanding change, you both have a better chance to be happy. If you treat any positive change as a bonus and not as a requirement, you're more likely to have a satisfying relationship.

Many couples who have been together for years have a love that in many ways is better than ever. They are grateful to be with each other and are excited about the future. Regardless of how long partners have been together, a large part of what makes a relationship great is consistently demonstrating respect and love for each other, while delighting in each other's presence.

18

Keeping the Fire Stoked

When you do your best to create and then sustain a fun and passionate relationship, you have a great chance of keeping the flames of your love burning brightly. It takes awareness, desire, time, and energy to keep your relationship satisfying for both of you, and it's well worth the effort.

ALTHOUGH SOME COUPLES make their relationship appear effortless and all seems well, behind the scenes one or both may miss what once made their lives together more exciting and satisfying. Emotional distance between partners can progress slowly and subtly, and thus may at first go unnoticed. Taking your partner and your relationship for granted will begin to weaken your strong bond. A relationship needs to be consistently nurtured or, like a garden that doesn't get enough water, sun, or soil, it will show signs of neglect.

Many people put a lot of time and energy into creating something special, but then ignore what it takes to sustain it. For example, let's say someone starts going to the gym on a regular basis. They get in very good shape and are feeling great. They might even take a few weeks off from their workouts and still look and feel good. However, if they stop working out for a prolonged period of time, signs of muscle weakness and overall fatigue will appear. If they want to continue receiving the benefits of their initial efforts, they'll have to continue working out, or they'll be back where they started. Similar to maintaining the gains made at the gym, it takes work to keep a relationship in great shape. It may not take the same amount of energy, time, and attention initially put forth, but it still takes willingness and effort.

It's not uncommon for a person to say or do something that's perceived as hurtful by their partner, who then experiences sadness, anger, or possibly a combination of these and other unpleasant feelings. The emotionally wounded person often believes that their partner has been insensitive to their needs, and they may express their feelings, dig their heels in and take a stand, or emotionally withdraw. Whatever the response, it often includes not reaching out to reconnect unless their partner apologizes or tries to make things better.

If you find yourself in this situation, instead of choosing not to approach your partner unless they come toward you, I recommend trying to communicate honestly and lovingly. Speak your truth and share your feelings, while being open to what your partner has to say. By acting in this way, you're doing your best to ensure that problems don't linger and possibly threaten your relationship.

Problems that stay hidden diminish the intensity of your connection. Since our goal is to keep the flames of love and passion burning brightly, bringing issues into the open and respectfully discussing your thoughts and feelings goes a long way toward resolving what might otherwise create an emotional distance between you.

Ignoring your partner's needs or failing to show appreciation for them will create an emotional separation that may lead your partner to look elsewhere for fulfillment. It doesn't necessarily mean that they'll have an affair or end the relationship, but they'll begin to feel unsatisfied, regardless of whether they admit it. Depending on their personality, it may be difficult to tell how they're feeling, as some people will not complain, argue, or fight, but will distance themselves emotionally and physically when they're unhappy. Don't assume that your partner is happy merely because they don't voice their unhappiness.

Books about how to save a relationship are normally read by those who believe that their relationship isn't satisfying and may be in danger of ending. There's often a sense of urgency and desperation for people reading these books. Although the advice may be helpful, it's painful to experience a distance from your partner and to confront the potential end of what was once very special. While it's possible that the relationship can improve, it will take a lot of work, and sadly it's often too late.

I encourage you to give regular attention to the health and happiness of your relationship. This is a much better option than constantly trying to repair what's damaged. When you take the lead in keeping the fire stoked, you prove yourself to be a caring, sensitive, and thoughtful lover. Your actions may very well ensure that there's never a reason to reach for a "how to save a relationship" book.

Knowing what keeps your partner satisfied and engaged is important. Some people thrive on sameness and routine. If this is what makes your partner happy, be consistent and consider subtle variations when doing whatever it is that brings them joy. For others, variety keeps things exciting. It's important to know what your partner desires, and to discuss what keeps each of you happy.

When trying to keep things fun and exciting, it's possible that you could be doing what has always worked before, but it no longer has the same impact. Desires can change over time, so avoid the mistake of making assumptions based on what may no longer be true. Also, be aware of the possibility that messages being sent aren't being received, or that one of you may want something that the other is no longer eager or willing to give. It's sad when a couple struggles, and frustrating when both people are trying hard, but it's not working.

Most people want to feel the joy that comes with being cared for and desired. One question to ask your partner that can help you determine how to bring them that joy is, "If I could tell you five things that would let you know how special you are to me and how much I care for and love you, what would they be?" When appropriate, I would write down their responses word for word, as it's very important to say what they would like to hear in the way that they would like to hear it.

You can also consider saying, "I want us to experience the excitement and passion that we felt when we first starting dating. What can we do to recapture or create those special feelings?" After asking this question, truly hear their responses rather than reacting defensively. If you respond only from the emotional pain you may experience when hearing what they say, you will be less able to recreate your initial passion. Remember that it takes work to keep the fire burning brightly, and it's worth it.

Are there things that you know you could do or say to keep things vibrant and passionate? Are you waiting for your partner to make the first move? I highly recommend taking the initiative. What gets the two of you excited? Is it time away from the daily routine? Is it vacations without connection to work, children, or other family members? Is it flowers, dinner at a special restaurant, a walk along the beach, or words of love? All of these may remind you how much you value each other and your relationship.

The actions that hopefully you take on your anniversary and Valentine's Day should be done often. Don't wait for the "right time." Consider giving a gift for no other reason than to express that you love and value your partner. You can do something special to acknowledge all that they do, and how fortunate you feel to be with them.

It's also important to be aware of what gets and keeps you satisfied. Sometimes we're good at asking others what they want and need, but we're not as good at asking ourselves what we need. If your partner asked you what they could do to keep you happy and excited, how would you respond? Which past experiences with your partner did you love? What new experiences might you enjoy? Part of your responsibility when it comes to keeping the fire stoked is to answer these questions and to be willing to share your desires.

Even when you have a close and strong connection that's built on a foundation of trust and love, the excitement that you experienced early on can diminish. A fire will not last forever unless you make the effort to keep it going. Keep the flames blazing, for if the fire dies, it may be very difficult or impossible to restart. It's much easier to tend a fire than to try to relight it after it's burned out.

Many people miss or don't heed the subtle or not-so-subtle signals that their partner wants or needs improvements in the relationship. Some people convince themselves that there's plenty of time to make changes and recapture what once was, or they think that if they ignore the warnings, the problems will just go away. These people are often shocked when their partner looks to someone else for emotional or physical connection, or ends the relationship.

When asked the reasons that they began an affair or ended a relationship, many people say that although they still love their partner, their desires for passion, excitement, and emotional fulfillment were not being met, and it had been too long since they were genuinely content. If the fire burns too low for too long, the bond between you will weaken. Do what it takes to keep your love alive and thriving.

I'm not saying that an affair is ever justified. Nor do I think that infidelity is inevitable, even when a couple struggles to be happy. What I do believe is that people are far less likely to stray if the fire is strong at home. Do what you can to keep your relationship satisfying and pleasurable, while speaking your truth and acting with integrity.

The good news is that keeping the fire stoked can be a lot of fun! Trying to please your partner and fulfill their needs by being playful, romantic, and sexual can be one of the most enjoyable parts of being together. When joined with a desire and willingness to make each other happy, your efforts will keep the fire going strong.

Honor each other and your relationship by being attentive and loving. When you consistently keep the fire stoked, it allows for a lifetime of passion and pleasure.

19

"Baby, You're the Best"

It's a great feeling when your partner tells you that they feel incredibly fortunate to be with you, and you satisfy their desires in a way that no one else ever has. Make the effort to keep your relationship fun and exciting, and consistently demonstrate your devotion with affection and love. When you do this, there's an excellent chance that your partner will say to you, "Baby, you're the best."

IMAGINE A COMPETITION in which there's a great prize that goes to the winner, and you're the only person who has a chance to win. If both of you are living up to your agreement to be in a committed, monogamous relationship, you have been given the opportunity to be the one and only participant in the contest to be your partner's best lover, ever.

Since you're the sole participant in this competition, it's easy to take your opportunity for granted, and to think that you don't have to work hard to win, or to do everything it takes to be the best. However, if you fail to make the effort, your partner may become dissatisfied. If your lack of effort continues for too long, they may be tempted to give someone else a chance to be the best.

Fortunately, there's a lot that you can do to give yourself an excellent chance to win, and in previous chapters we discussed many of these things. None of us is or should be expected to be perfect, but I do hope that you will communicate honestly and openly, and do what you can to keep your relationship happy and thriving. If you do your best and things don't work out, at least it won't be for lack of effort, and you will have learned a great deal that will serve you in your next relationship. Hopefully, the one you're in is right for both of you, and you're doing what it takes to keep it loving, satisfying, and fun.

Being the best doesn't mean that in every way, shape, and form you're better than everyone else. It doesn't mean that you need to outshine everyone else in everything you do and say. It means that in the totality of how you treat and communicate with your partner, you're the best for them.

Whenever possible, share with your partner the many ways they're so very special. They may be the best provider, parent, kisser, or listener. They may be the most caring, thoughtful, and sensitive person you've ever met, or they may have any of a hundred different qualities that make them wonderful.

When the time is right, and it usually is, tell them about the great qualities that make them the best. You may want to elaborate by saying something like, "You give the greatest hugs, and when you hold me I feel safe and loved," or "You're the best listener. When I speak, you genuinely hear and understand what I have to say." When you add, "No one else has ever done this the way you do," or "I'm continually amazed at how great you are at _____," you'll take your relationship to another level.

Remember that it's easier for a heart to close than it is to open, so choose your words carefully. Rather than saying, "You're the best at taking out the garbage," you could say, "All the seemingly small things you do make a big difference to me." Instead of saying, "You're the best dishwasher," you could say, "I appreciate it very much when you wash the dishes. It makes me feel cared for and respected."

If you're not getting along, think about your part in creating tension in your relationship. When you're ready to take responsibility for your words and actions, and to communicate calmly without blaming your partner, it will be time to speak your truth. If appropriate, I recommend apologizing for your role in creating any distance between you. Remember that nonverbal communication is often more important than the words that you use. When apologizing, be truthful, and use a sincere and respectful tone.

Let your partner know the many ways in which they make you feel great when you're being physically intimate with each other. Most people thrive when hearing that they're beyond compare. Sometimes, details are better left unspoken, and all that needs to be said is, "The way you do _____ is amazing. Baby, you're the best."

If you've had companions in the past, when giving compliments to your current love, don't mention names or make comparisons. No one wants to hear, "Compared with _____, you're great" or "This other person was great at _____, but you do it better." While your intention may be to give a compliment, those types of comparisons can be unpleasant. I believe that there's no reason to talk about a previous companion when you're in the bedroom.

Be cautious about idolizing a former partner, which inevitably will make your current partner feel uncomfortable, and put them in the position of believing that they can never measure up, which can be demoralizing.

If your partner is your first and only love, don't say, "You're great, but I don't have anyone else to compare you to" or "You do that wonderfully, but what do I know." If you find yourself trying to tell your partner that they're wonderful, but realize that you've been inappropriate or hurtful, apologize immediately and then in a sincere, loving, and respectful way, restate what you really meant to say.

It's exciting to discover what makes your partner the best for you. Remember that neither of you has to be perfect at everything in order to be ideal for each other. Your partner is probably very special in many ways, and it's possible that you haven't taken enough time to think about and share with them all the ways in which they shine. Rather than pointing out their weaknesses or inadequacies, or saying that you wish things were different, telling them what makes them a great partner is a wonderful way to express your love.

When you focus on all your companion's good and great qualities, it will be easy to tell them how amazing they are. When you tell them that they're the best, you provide another opportunity for them to feel really good about themselves. Part of being your partner's best lover, ever, is taking the time to communicate how fortunate you are to have them in your life.

Some people are good at acknowledging others for their fine qualities, but they're not good at accepting compliments. They may have been taught to deflect praise, or they may genuinely think that they're not deserving of it. If you're one of these people, it's important to be receptive to your partner's compliments. You may come to understand how certain character traits that come naturally to you make you desirable. For example, you may find that qualities you take for granted, such as being kind, thoughtful, and considerate, are the very qualities that make you very special to your partner.

It's also important to honor what you think are your fine qualities, even if your partner doesn't seem to appreciate them. It's worth asking your partner if what you consider to be special about yourself is important to them. Their response will help you better understand their needs and values.

How often should you tell your partner that they're desirable? As long as you do it at the right time and in the right way, it's hard to express your admiration too often. I encourage you to tell your partner frequently and sincerely how good you feel in their presence and how much you love them.

If you're looking for ways to be your partner's best lover, ever, consider what we have previously discussed. In earlier chapters I wrote about how to express your emotions in a loving and respectful way, and about how to truly hear what your partner is saying. We discussed the benefits of giving up the need to be right, offering sincere compliments, being kind, and sharing plenty of quality time with your partner.

We talked about the importance of speaking your truth, living up to your agreements, and living with integrity. We addressed meeting each other's needs as much as possible, which includes the desires for non-sexual and sexual intimacy. We discussed the many ways that you can express your love for your partner. We talked about acceptance, appreciating your partner, and the importance of keeping the flames of your love burning brightly.

I honor your desire to be a lover of the highest quality. I encourage you to let your partner know how wonderful they are and how much you cherish your relationship. Through your words, touch, actions, and ways of being, you can demonstrate how much you appreciate and love them. I have great confidence that you can and will experience the joy that comes from hearing your partner say, "You're the best lover, ever."

Acknowledgments

THIS BOOK WOULDN'T have been written without the love, support, and encouragement of many people.

Thank you to my partner, Barbara, for her inspiration and loving heart.

Thank you to my daughter, Maya, who allows me the special joy of being a father to a wonderful woman, and who wisely told me that since I don't make my living from writing, I have the freedom to write what I want.

I thank my mom, dad, sisters, brothers-in-law, nephew, cousins and aunts and uncles, whom I love so much.

I thank my Warrior brothers in The Mankind Project, who supported and encouraged me.

Thank you to the Mos and their partners, the men and women who have been my closest friends for most of my life.

Many thanks to Rose for helping me own my gifts and for encouraging me to express them; Eric for keeping me accountable to my commitment to writing; Dawn for her support and friendship; Peggy for her encouragement;

Sylvia for modeling true devotion; and Rex for inspiring me with his strength and resilience.

Thank you to Jesse, Erin, Peter, Rony, Kendra, and all the talented people at Page Two Strategies for helping me take my book past the finish line.

To Lenny and David, my chiropractors, thank you so much for keeping my spine, extremities, and nerve system functioning at their best.

To all the lovers in the world, I thank you!

Made in the USA
Las Vegas, NV
01 February 2022